AI
CAME TO HIM

A Practical Biblical Guide To Divine Healing

BY

BOB WHITE

GENC1V3 MINISTRIES

ISBN 978-1-958788-81-3 (Digital)

ISBN 978-1-958788-87-5 (Paperback)

ISBN 978-1-958788-88-2 (Hardcover)

Publify Publishing

1412 W. Ave B

Lampasas, TX 76550

publifypublishing@gmail.com

Contents

INTRODUCTION

H ealing is one of the most debated subjects within the Christian faith. The question is, does God want everyone healed or does He want some healed and some sick? The Bible explicitly states that God is no respecter of one person over another in Acts 10:34,

> Then Peter began to speak: "I now realize how true
> it is that God does not show favoritism."

You can break that scripture down in the Greek, word by word, and any other way that you want to, but it truly means that God does not esteem one person over another. What He does for one person, He will do for another.

People will argue this. They will talk about how God made them sick or how He has allowed them to be sick to fulfill His will. They will cite their experience and the experiences of others. They will fight like the dickens to make sure that they ensure their right to be sick and then blame it on God.

I wholeheartedly disagree with these people and believe them to be unknowing tools of the enemy. Just as when Peter took Jesus aside in Matthew 16:22-23 and rebuked him for saying that he would suffer, be killed by the Pharisees, and resurrected. Jesus replied as follows,

> Peter took Him aside and began to rebuke Him. "Far be it from You, Lord!" he said. "This shall never happen to You!" But Jesus turned and said to Peter, "Get behind Me, Satan! You are a stumbling block to Me. For you do not have in mind the things of God, but the things of men."

Jesus wasn't calling Peter, Satan. He knew where the words spoken by Peter had come from. They had come from the pit of Hell. Without Jesus laying down His life, there would be no remission of sins. And without the resurrection, then death, Hell and the grave would still rule. Peter's words sounded noble and friendly on the surface, but they were at cross purposes with God's will. That is exactly what happens when we as Christians share our experiences and preach from those experiences rather than sharing and preaching God's Word. God's Word is inspired and anointed. Our experiences are only inspired and anointed as they line up with God's Word. People will ask, "Are you saying that I don't have enough faith?" Well, maybe I am. But I am most definitely saying that your lack or my lack of healing is not because God made you sick or allowed you to be sick. Romans 8:28 states,

And we know that in all things God works for the good of those who love him, who have been called according to his purpose.

This means that God will make anything and everything work for your good if you love Him, even sickness. But that does not mean that He caused your sickness. Yes, He allows it, but He allows it because you have either not followed His Word or have broken one of His immutable laws. God is sovereign, but that does not mean that every situation you find yourself in is because He ordained it. It is because He allowed it for one of many different reasons. In this book, I have attempted to touch upon some of those possible reasons..

God wants us well. Jesus died and took our sins upon himself so that all men might be saved. Are all men saved? No, they are not. Why? The primary reason is because they do not believe in the Gospel and on Jesus' work at the cross or on His resurrection. God wants us all healed. I challenge you to find one place in the New Testament where Jesus did not heal "all who came to Him." Are all healed? No, they are not. Why? Since this is part of the Gospel (Good News) one would suspect that it is because they do not believe in the Gospel about healing and the work that Jesus performed by taking our sicknesses on the whipping post. For it states in 1 Peter 2:24,

> "Who Himself bore our sins" in His body on the tree, so that, having been dead to sins, we might live to righteousness. "By whose scourge marks you have been healed."

If you suspect that it is because people do not believe, then you are correct. I will discuss in depth herein some of the reasons why some don't find healing and some don't experience health. I will also discuss some of the many ways in which we can assure ourselves that we walk in the divine health that God intends for us.

So, for those that don't know me, but may find themselves disagreeing with me straight out of the box as to healing, I will share those tenets of scripture that I believe we, as Believers, must hold to. I allude often to Alistair Begg's quote that, "The main things are the plain things, and the plain things are the main things." The major tenets of scripture that I allude to, I will list herein. I will not elaborate extensively on them. If you do not hold to these tenets, then I suggest that you re-examine your salvation. I have left out items that I believe are very clearly tenets of scripture but would only create contention and strife among some of those who read this book. I have no issue or problem with us disagreeing. I, however, am focusing on the issue of healing herein and I truly believe that it would prove counterproductive to include those issues which I believe are likely highly contentious issues. Although I have perfect confidence in my scriptural stance, I also believe that these contentious issues would only distract from my main focus here, which is healing. Therefore, I have only included, below, the items that a person's eternal salvation and basic Christian beliefs need to be based upon:

1. The virgin birth of Jesus Christ.

2. The incarnation of Jesus Christ (fully man and fully God).

3. Jesus Christ is God's only begotten (reproduced directly by the seed of the Holy Spirit) Son.

4. Jesus died and was buried. He was resurrected by the power of the Holy Spirit on the third day. He descended into Hell to take the keys to death, Hell, and the grave from the enemy. He returned to Earth and was seen by His disciples and others for 40 days and then ascended into the Heavenlies and is now seated at the right hand of God the Father Almighty.

5. There is one God, and that one God exists in three persons – the Father, the Son, and the Holy Spirit.

6. While all Believers may have diverse theological teachings based upon what church or school they attended, we, as Believers, should hold to the belief that the Bible is the inspired (Holy Spirit) and infallible (inerrant) Word of God. This may not lead us to the same beliefs, but it certainly can and should lead us to a point in which we can call one another brothers and sisters in the faith.

7. With the understanding, as stated by Jesus to Nicodemus in John 3:7b, that "we must be born again," our spirits must receive the regeneration of the Holy Spirit. In the Garden when they sinned, Adam and Eve were told that they would surely die, and they did, spiritually and physically. There is no spiritual life and thus death reigns without this rebirth spoken of in John 3:7.

8. The Holy Spirit then seals us, so that we are eternally assured of our salvation. No one in Heaven, Hell, or on Earth can take what the Holy Spirit has sealed.

9. There is only one way to be saved (delivered, set free) and that is through Jesus Christ and we are saved by grace (unmerited favor) through faith, not by works.

10. Jesus will return to take unto Himself all that are His. There will ultimately be a final judgment. Those whose names are found written in the Lamb's Book of Life will reside eternally with God. Those whose names are not found in the Lamb's Book of Life (or Book of Life, the same) will reside forever with Satan (the Adversary) in the lake of fire.

CHAPTER ONE

WHAT DOES THE BIBLE SAY ABOUT HEALING?

This, to me, is the ultimate question concerning healing. There is no basis to believe in someone's knowledge no matter how great or extensive it may be. No matter whether they be a medical doctor (MD), Neurosurgeon, Psychiatrist, etc., that has studied that specific aspect of medicine for decades. Their knowledge is limited and based on the wisdom of scientific observation. Don't misunderstand what I am saying. I thank God for the limited knowledge that doctors have and for some of the medications, surgical procedures, neurological knowledge, and revelations of the human psyche which have been discovered over the years. I have said it before and I will say it again, this is not a book that is anti-medicine. It is a book that is pro-biblical healing. God created us. It is Him and Him alone that knows exactly how we function – physically, emotionally, mentally, and spiritually.

I believe that the Bible is the inerrant word of God. And, as time goes on, it has been proven so through, not only medical science, but also through various aspects of astronomy, archaeology, geology, and other branches of science, to be, as previously stated, inerrant. If there appears to be a conflict between a known scientific fact and a biblical revelation, then there is either a misinterpretation of scientific fact or a misinterpretation of the Bible, because the two should always match. There is no situation or scenario where that is not true. There are two things that scientists should never do: 1) Re-interpret theological facts to match scientific facts; and 2) Twist scientific facts to match their world view, even if the facts are obviously contrary to their world view. There are also two similar things that theologians should never do: 1) Re-interpret scientific facts to match theological facts; and 2) Twist scientific facts to match their world view. Unfortunately, these two things happen a lot in today's cancel culture and politically correct society. That is some of what leads to the disinformation and the apparent dichotomy between science and biblical Christianity. Note I did not say religion.

There is one singular piece of written material that holds the sincere and absolute truth and that is God's Word. That Word is the Holy Bible. There are many other pieces of literature used by other religions. That too is what adds to the confusion between science and God's Word. Where do these books come from? I posit that many are demonically influenced and produced by those that follow the fallen angels who have called themselves "gods" throughout time since the angelic fall. Not just in this age, but in all ages (thousands of years). All eras (millions of years). All eons (billions of years). Just as I am sure that I will upset some scientifically trained individuals with my stance on the Bible being the one sure and absolute truth, I am just as sure that I will upset some Christian theologically trained individuals by referring to millions and even billions of years with relation to the Earth. This is one of those areas in which I believe that a little more study and a little less rigidity on the Christian side would lead to a verifiable and certifiable answer in which the scientific facts and biblical facts would line up quite nicely. An area where the scientists may want to spend a little more time in study, would be with regard to the items that they call "biblical myths" and areas that are referred to as "myths" with regard to other locations and ages. Both sets of scholars may be stunned at what they could learn, if they would open their minds to God's Word and His wisdom (the Bible). If you have never read the Bible, then how can you intelligently discuss it? You can't. Read the Bible first and other books in which the author is not afraid to address the aforementioned, discord and dichotomy, as I have done in my book, "Unseen War," which sheds some light on some of the areas that I discuss herein.

The above paragraph may seem like a rabbit trail that I chose to take that had little, if anything, to do with healing. My point was and is, that no matter what the item of discussion may be, there is only one foundational basis of truth about that item, and that foundation is the Bible. If you don't approach the item from that viewpoint, then you have absolutely no chance to determine truth. Keeping that in mind as well as what it states in Romans 10:17, *"faith comes by hearing and hearing by the Word of God,"* let's continue to look at what else the Bible states concerning healing.

1. First off, God desires that man live and not die. We were created with a disposition toward death. Sin entered and man experienced death. Death was and is experienced in every aspect of our being – physical, emotional, mental, and spiritual. All of these aspects of death (death is separation from life – "life" is God) work on the human body. Humans were immediately cut-off from God spiritually. We died spiritually immediately, when Adam sinned. That disobedience separated us from God's presence and thus from "life" itself. God had breathed life into Adam which in Hebrew is referred to as the *"Nishmat chaim."* This refers to the Holy Spirit of God. In other words, when God gave man life, it was via the Holy Spirit that life sprang forth and man's spirit lived and thus the spirit gave life to all the other aspects of his being – both his soul and body. When the spirit died the rest of the men also began to perish and from that time until now there have only been two men that lived who have avoided the fate of physical death. Those two men are Enoch (Genesis 5:22-24) and Elijah (2 Kings 2:11). The relationship of men with death changed due to the work of Christ on the cross and His resurrection. As Jesus stated to Martha in John 11:25-26,

Jesus said to her, "I am the resurrection and the life. The one who believes in me will live, even though they die; and whoever lives by believing in me will never die. Do you believe this?"

Do you believe this? Well, do you? That question entails the basis of all life and death.

2. God also desires that man experience wholeness. The word used for "salvation" within the Bible in the Greek is *soteria*. The NAS New Testament Greek Lexicon identifies the word as being used to convey "deliverance, preservation, safety, salvation." So, when it speaks of a man being "saved" in the New Testament, there is more to it than just that person being assured of not going to Hell. Don't get me wrong. That is assuredly a very important aspect of receiving Christ or being saved, but it is not all that was meant to be conveyed to the one that receives Christ. God's intent is that we be delivered from the attacks of the enemy; that we be preserved through all the enemy's attacks; that we be safe through life; and that we experience the saving power of God in all that we do up until we are called to our Heavenly home. This undoubtedly includes physical healing. Those of you who would try to spiritualize this and try to say that it has to do with the saving of the soul only, I suppose, intend to come back with Jesus wearing the body that you currently have. That is not what the Bible states. The New Testament tells us that we can be "saved" and then proceeds to tell us how to walk in that salvation. This includes physical healing. Those that Jesus healed during

His ministry were healed under the Old Covenant and not the New Covenant. The New Covenant began after His death and resurrection. As stated in Hebrews 8:13,

By speaking of a new covenant, He has made the first one obsolete; and what is obsolete, and aging will soon disappear.

The writer of Hebrews also clarified the ministry of Jesus and compared the two covenants in Hebrews 13:1,

Now, however, Jesus has received a much more excellent ministry, just as the covenant He mediates is better and is founded on better promises.

So, if Jesus has received "a much more excellent ministry" and if the new covenant is founded on "better promises." Wouldn't it stand to reason that the Jesus that it states in various and sundry places in the New Testament "healed all who came to Him" would still want them all healed? Or did the proclaimed "new covenant" and "better promises" fall short? Did the one who "healed all who came to Him" suddenly change His mind? Well, let's see Hebrews 13:8 states that *"Jesus Christ is the same yesterday and today and forever."* Based on this information, the answer would seem to be that God wants us whole and that would include physical healing.

3. We live in the temple of the Holy Spirit. As stated above, when we became born again that same Spirit of God that was removed from us when Adam fell has been restored to us. We have been restored to how God originally created mankind. God sits on the throne of our lives.

David Wilkerson once stated that we would always have a Christ on the throne of our lives. It will either be the Antichrist (Beast) or Jesus Christ (Messiah). As noted in 1 Corinthians 6:19,

Do you not know that your bodies are temples of the Holy Spirit, who is in you, whom you have received from God? You are not your own;

As temples of the Holy Spirit, God has stated that we are not our own. We belong to Him and are His residence in this sphere. So, let me ask, "How do you care for your house?" When it gets run down, the paint is bad, the structural framework fails, termites attack it, or the plumbing fails, do you just say, "Oh well, that is just the nature of things" and go about your business. No, if you are a good steward, even though "moth and rust destroy," you repair your home for you have to live in it. You make it the best that you can. So, what you say is the God who spared no expense on an earthly tabernacle will just allow His human temple to corrode and rust away – to be destroyed by sickness and disease until it is not livable anymore.

I can hear many of you saying, "Well, we do get old and die." I will not argue that. We still live in a fallen world. Our bodies, though redeemed, have not yet been restored. But that does not mean that God leaves us at the mercy of Satan and his demonic horde and his list of diseases and sicknesses with no recourse. Romans 8:11 states,

And if the Spirit of him who raised Jesus from the dead is living in you, He who raised Christ from the dead will also give life to your mortal bodies because of his Spirit who lives in you.

The word "life" in this passage is the Greek word *zóopoieó*, which means "to make alive." Literally, it means "to make that which was dead to live." It is the same word used in Romans 4:17b, "*the God who gives life to the dead and calls into being things that were not.*" What does the Bible say of Caleb who chose to believe and follow God and who states in Joshua 14:10-11?

> Now then, just as the LORD promised, He has kept me alive for forty-five years since the time He said this to Moses, while Israel moved about in the wilderness. So here I am today, eighty-five years old! I am still as strong today as the day Moses sent me out; I'm just as vigorous to go out to battle now as I was then.

Caleb obeyed God and believed His report not the report of the other ten spies. He believed what God spoke. He believed God's Word. The problem is not whether or not God will restore our health. Our bodies are His temple. It is absurd to think that you would take better care of your house than He would these living houses He possesses. The Bible states, as much. The problem is that, like the other spies, we either don't obey, we don't believe, or both. God's heart is to restore us, His living abode, as stated in 1 Corinthians 3:16,

> Don't you know that you yourselves are God's temple and that God's Spirit dwells in your midst?

4. In John 14:31, Jesus states that He "does exactly" what He sees the Father doing. He then goes on in John 15 to explain that we can also do what Jesus does by "abiding" in Him. This is to be accomplished by, as is stated in verse 14, "doing what He commands." Which, in short, is to, "love one another." This means that we also would do what the Father does. Acts 10:38 states,

> How God anointed Jesus of Nazareth with the Holy Spirit and power, and how He went around doing good and healing all who were under the power of the devil, because God was with him.

What then does the Father clearly do as shown in this short verse? First, He empowers us. We do not empower ourselves. We are empowered by His Holy Spirit and power. Second, He went around doing good. That was His primary objective, to do good through Christ Jesus. Third, He healed "all" who were under the power of the Devil. He didn't just heal a few, not just some, not almost all, but rather "all." May His will be done on earth as it is in Heaven. Fourth, God was "always" with Him (Jesus). So, let's get this right. He was always doing good because the Father was always with Him. This meant that He was always healing "all." Or, in a different vernacular, "everyone." What was Jesus' will for us? To do the will of the Father. How often did He want us to do that? Always. Which means that He wants us to pray for everyone to be healed always and He will empower us to do that as stated in John 15:7,

> If you remain in me and my words remain in you, ask whatever you wish, and it will be done for you.

There is no logical argument that can be presented to prove that God does not want us healed. And, if He wants us healed, then what is preventing us from being healed?

5. *But Christ has indeed been raised from the dead, the first fruits of those who have fallen asleep. For since death came through a man, the resurrection of the dead comes also through a man. For as in Adam all die, so in Christ all will be made alive. But each in his own turn: Christ the firstfruits; then at His coming, those who belong to Him.*

1 Corinthians 15:20-23

Not only did death come through a man but then sickness and disease also came with death. If there is no death, then there is no sickness nor disease. Some theologians believe that there was sickness and disease prior to Adam's fall. They posit that otherwise, how is the fossil record which definitely shows fossils of dead humanoid creatures (Neanderthal, Cro-Magnon, Denisovan, etc.) and fossils of dead animals rectified? To the true creationist, the explanation is simple in that they advance that the fossilized record and death is due to Noah's flood and thus death that occurred prior to the flood occurred after the curse of Adam. What I refer to as the true creationist is the person who believes that all physical creation from the edge of the universe to the edge of the universe was created in six 24-hour days before God rested on the seventh day. All the items associated with death and the fossil record, etc. are due to the massive upheaval which happened during the flood that occurred in Noah's lifetime. This upheaval included massive earthquakes, volcanic eruptions, and water springing forth from within the Earth itself (the "great deep").

Geologists, based on carbon dating, insist that the Earth is much older than the approximate 6,000 years of age that a true creationist believes the Earth is. There are some theologians that hold to the view that while the Earth was created by God that the Earth is indeed older than the 6,000 years of age of which a true creationist holds to. While all of this is very interesting, I am sure some of you are wondering why I am spending so much time expounding upon it in a book about physical healing.

I ask you to pause momentarily and reflect on the impact that these beliefs have on the issues of death, sickness, and disease in conjunction with God's desire to keep us healthy. Let's review for a moment:

1) The stance of the true creationist lines up nicely with the assumed fact that God wants His people well because death, sickness, and disease all showed up at the same time – after Adam's fall. This does not alleviate the ongoing debate between creationists and scientists, as to the age of the Earth and the many other science/ theological debates that are ongoing. There is no consensus to the truth here, due to the conflict related.

2) So, if the Earth is indeed older than the true creationist asserts, then the creation of the Earth in six days is brought into question, as is the inerrancy of not only these scriptures, but all of the rest. I mean, if you can't believe beyond a shadow of a doubt one part of scripture, how do you intend to determine which parts of scripture

can be believed and which parts are merely the recounting of a fable, myth, or history as remembered by the Jews. Therefore, there is no consensus regarding scripture and science once again.

3) But what if both were true? What if the Earth that we live on was not only brought back to life (re-created) in six days, but in six 24-hour days? What if there is not and has never been any conflict between the theology of creation and the science of creation? If those two items are true and in agreement, then God's Word is not just true, but inerrantly true. Thus, meaning that He not only wants you not dead, but also not sick or diseased. "*Your kingdom come, Your will be done on earth, as it is in Heaven.*"

4) My previous book, "Unseen War," covers this issue in depth and detail. If you want a more detailed coverage of this issue, then please read *Unseen War* concerning this. But less detail is needed to support my premise herein. Just because the Bible does not clearly state the fact that the Earth, as currently created, is literally 6,000 plus years old does not mean that it is not. Nor does the fact that the Bible does not state succinctly that the Earth is possibly millions or even billions of years old does it not mean that it is not and that the scientific data is not correct?

5) What theologians are missing is what the focus of the Bible is. The Bible's only focus is the redemption and salvation of mankind in this age. That means that the focus is Jesus, and then Jesus, and then after that, Jesus.

Some items that would be distractions simply are not covered in greater detail.

6) What scientists are missing is that they are totally ignoring and passing off as myth the items that are biblically spelled out. If you dig into the Hebrew language, I believe that it is clear that the six days were a recreation of some things and a creation of others. But what is definitively clear is that the Earth itself was already here – *"now the earth was formless and void."* How long had it been formless and void? Why was it formless and void? Most secular scientists wouldn't know because most will not look past their bias to ask relevant questions.

7) If the Earth was not only here, but was previously inhabited in other ages by other creations, then there is no issue with the age of the Earth, the dinosaurs, the fossil record, other humanoid creatures, etc. They are all God's creation.

8) Finally, did Adam bring death, sickness, and disease into this age by his fall from grace? Yes. To that age. That is what the Bible teaches beyond a shadow of a doubt.

9) Was there death on Earth prior to Adam's fall? Yes. During former ages, which are alluded to in the scriptures. This can be found when your study focus is on former ages and other associated areas. This is validated by the fossil record. To have fossils, you must have dead organisms.

10) Both the Prophet Isaiah (Isaiah 25:8) and Apostle Paul (1 Corinthians 15:54) clearly state, "death is swallowed up in

victory." Meaning that death shall be vanquished. Done away with. Overcome at the end of this age. It is clear that as we live out our lives during the Millennial period, there will be for all intents no death, no sickness, and no disease. Satan will have been imprisoned and held in the Abyss.

11) Thus, where does death, sickness, and disease come from? Clearly it emanates from Satan, as is simply stated in Acts 10:38,

> Jesus from Nazareth, how God anointed Him with the Holy Spirit and with power, who went about doing good and healing all those being oppressed by the devil, because God was with Him.

So, what should you take from this? Simply that sin and therewith death, disease, and sickness have followed Satan (the Adversary) through the many years that he has battled not just God, but God's chosen in each age and generation. There has obviously been much death as can be adjudged by the fossil records and based on the fact that everything and everyone (other than Enoch and Elijah) has died or will die during this current age. God created and recreated in each age, just as He will in the Millennium, practically sans death, sickness, and disease. But the unleashing of the Adversary has always been the harbinger of sin and then sickness, disease, and death. There will be those living in the Millennium that lived through the Tribulation and who will continue to produce offspring, etc. Isaiah 65:20 relates the following to them,

Never again will there be in it an infant who lives but a few days, or an old man who does not live out his years; the one who dies at a hundred will be thought a mere child; the one who fails to reach a hundred will be considered accursed.

Meaning that sin, thus sickness and disease and death will be minimized, but the Adamic nature will still be a part of those born of the flesh. These will have to receive Christ as those of us that have received our eternal bodies did in the preceding age.

In the Age of the New Jerusalem there will be no death, disease, or sickness associated with any aspect of that Age. We will be with the Lord and will dwell with Him forevermore. "Lord, your will be done on earth as it is in Heaven." Divine healing is yours. Battle for it.

CHAPTER TWO

———◆———

WHY DO PEOPLE GET SICK?

T here are many reasons that people get sick. I will only cover seven reasons that I feel are main areas in this book. Some are physical, some mental, some emotional, and some genetic, but all sicknesses have their root in the spiritual realm. Sickness is merely the lack of life. God told Adam and Eve, if they ate from the Tree of the Knowledge of Good and Evil, that they would surely die and they did. They were separated from the source of life in the spirit and thus their physical beings began to deteriorate as their spiritual selves and souls fell further and further away from the source of life itself, God. Sickness and disease manifest themselves in many ways. Sicknesses and diseases can take on different names, but ultimately, they all share the same common denominator, death.

In all simplicity, what salvation, *soteria*, in the Greek means, is completeness and wholeness. That is what salvation in Christ is. We are reborn via the Holy Spirit into life, completeness, and wholeness. God breathes His breath (the Holy Spirit) into us, just as He originally did to Adam and Eve and this dead lump of clay once again lives. Death no longer holds sway over us. Life dwells within us by the Holy Spirit. We are healed and whole – spirit, soul, and body.

Then, why do people continue to get sick?

One, our bodies are still fallen. Jesus has won a clear victory in the spiritual realm, but He does not finalize His victory in the physical realm until He returns with the saints at Armageddon. Sometime before that, we, the Believers, will receive new, glorified physical bodies either at the rapture (*harpazo*, catching away) or after they arrive in the heavens from the Tribulation. Some say that it is at Jesus' second coming that we receive our new bodies. I don't find that belief bears up under scrutiny. First off, we are with Jesus at His second coming in Revelation 19. We comprise the armies of Heaven along with the angelic host. Jesus returns in His glorified body to a physical world, just as we return to a physical world with Him in our glorified bodies. Many don't believe in a "catching away." I find that it is incomprehensible after a thorough study of the scriptures to not believe in a catching away or "rapture." Paul states in 1 Thessalonians 4:16-18,

> For the Lord himself shall descend from Heaven with a shout, with the voice of the archangel, and with the trump of God: and the dead in Christ shall

rise first: Then we which are alive and remain shall be caught up together with them in the clouds, to meet the Lord in the air: and so shall we ever be with the Lord. Wherefore comfort one another with these words.

"Well," you may say, "that does not mention new bodies." 1 Corinthians 15:51-53 certainly mentions new bodies and it also speaks of the trumpet and some being alive and some dead at that time,

Listen, I tell you a mystery: We will not all sleep, but we will all be changed—in an instant, in the twinkling of an eye, at the last trumpet. For the trumpet will sound, the dead will be raised imperishable, and we will be changed. For the perishable must be clothed with the imperishable, and the mortal with immortality.

One can perform deeper studies concerning the Hebrew feasts. Specifically, the Feast of Trumpets and the similarity of Revelation 4:1 to the trumpet call and the fact that the Church is no longer mentioned after this trumpet. Why? Because the church is with Jesus in the Third Heaven. I will move along now since this is merely an aside with regards to having glorified bodies and when we might have them.

Two, some people get sick and stay sick because they don't believe God desires to heal them. They put more stock in their experience than they do in God's Word. I mean if you have no basis of truth, then what do you believe? If God's

Word is not clear that He desires all healed or if you do not believe that His Word is immutable and irrefutable, then you build your house on sand. You have no foundation for your faith. You are as is stated in James 1:6-8, a double-minded man who will receive nothing from God,

> But he must ask in faith, without doubting, because he who doubts is like a wave of the sea, blown and tossed by the wind. That man should not expect to receive anything from the Lord. He is a double-minded man, unstable in all his ways.

I mean, do you believe that you are going to get a specific word every time God wants to heal you and another word every time He does not want to heal you? God has sent His Word and healed us, as stated in Psalm 107:20, "*He sent out His word and healed them; He rescued them from the grave.*" There is your word. In Matthew 12:15, 19:2, and 21:4, He healed them all. There is your word.

Three, unbelievers and children oftentimes get sick because they are not protected. They are not sanctified (set apart unto God). Many of you will decry this statement. But I will point you to 1 Corinthians 7:14, which states,

> For the unbelieving husband has been sanctified through his wife, and the unbelieving wife has been sanctified through her believing husband. Otherwise, your children would be unclean, but as it is, they are holy.

The word translated as unclean comes from *a kaitharo* which literally means "not clean." This is the same word used in Revelation 17:4 which is translated there when referring to the Great Prostitute in the NIV as "filth." The use of that word to refer to demons and fallen angels is in 23 places in the Gospels, Acts, and the Revelation.

There is an interesting interlude with Jesus and the people in Luke 13:1-4,

> At that time some of those present told Jesus about the Galileans whose blood Pilate had mixed with their sacrifices. To this He replied, "Do you think that these Galileans were worse sinners than all the other Galileans, because they suffered this fate? No, I tell you. But unless you repent, you too will all perish. Or those eighteen who were killed when the tower of Siloam collapsed on them: Do you think that they were more sinful than all the others living in Jerusalem? No, I tell you. But unless you repent, you too will all perish."

It is interesting in that the people, as would the people in our day, expected Jesus to commiserate and empathize with those that died. But He actually told them that they too would potentially perish in like manner if they did not repent and come to God. What He was saying is that they had no protection. God is our protector and as you wander around in this unclean world full of uncleanness yourself (if unsaved), you are ultimately going to come across some situation or a demonic or fallen entity that carries out John 10:10 for the enemy. For there, it states that he (the enemy) came only to "*kill, steal, and destroy.*"

We are cleansed and sanctified by the blood of Christ and if you are not a Believer and even if you are a small child and your parents aren't Believers, then you have no protection. Some of you may not believe this because it runs crosswise with your belief in who God is. Sin separates. Redemption in Christ joins.

In Matthew 13:36-42 in the Parable of the Weeds (Tares) He explains even in more depth,

> Then Jesus dismissed the crowds and went into the house. His disciples came to Him and said, "Explain to us the parable of the weeds in the field." He replied, "The One who sows the good seed is the Son of Man. The field is the world, and the good seed represents the sons of the kingdom. The weeds are the sons of the evil one, and the enemy who sows them is the devil. The harvest is the end of the age, and the harvesters are angels. As the weeds are collected and burned in the fire, so will it be at the end of the age. The Son of Man will send out His angels, and they will weed out of His kingdom every cause of sin and all who practice lawlessness. And they will throw them into the fiery furnace, where there will be weeping and gnashing of teeth. Then the righteous will shine like the sun in the kingdom of their Father. He who has ears, let him hear.

The weeds or tares are who? They are the sons of the evil one. They do not know God nor have they ever known him. They were not and are not sanctified. There is no protection for them anywhere by anyone. Still, some of these get saved and become protected. The shame is when those who are born protected (due to their parents' beliefs) end up as tares (due to their unbelief) and unprotected. You can believe as you desire, but if your belief does not line up with what God states in His Word your faith is of no consequence. As stated in John 17:17, "*Sanctify them by the truth; your word is truth.*"

Four, people live in anxiety and stress. It is no secret that stress and anxiety have a massive negative impact on the body's immune system. The more you worry the greater your chance of getting sick. Some of you will state that that is the way you are. Then ask God to change you. You were once sinners until you got hold of the truth of the Gospel of Jesus Christ. A Christian has no excuse to worry or be anxious. As is clearly stated in Philippians 4:6-7,

> Be anxious for nothing, but in everything, by prayer and petition, with thanksgiving, present your requests to God. And the peace of God, which surpasses all understanding, will guard your hearts and your minds in Christ Jesus.

This is a command, "*Be anxious for nothing.*" To be anxious about things and to stress over them is an insult to God and a sin. It tells Him that you do not believe He can handle the situation. It not only stresses you, but it makes you double-minded and puts you in position, as stated in James 1:7, "*to receive nothing from God.*"

Stress causes you to revert from a position of confidence to a position of fear. 1 John 4:18 states,

> There is no fear in love. But perfect love drives out fear because fear has to do with punishment. The one who fears is not made perfect in love.

According to the American Psychological Society, stress can reduce the number of natural killer cells or lymphocytes in the body, which are needed to fight viruses. Put your trust in God and reduce your level of stress and anxiety over time to zero.

Five, some disease, just like some sin, is genetically driven. Now, I believe as Believers that we have been redeemed from any genetic curse and just as we were delivered from sin by the work that Jesus performed on the cross, we were also delivered from sickness and disease. There are a number of scriptures in the Old Testament that allude to the fact that YHWH stated that He would punish the sins of the Father on their children and grandchildren to the third and fourth generations. Those scriptures include Exodus 20:5; Numbers 14:18; and Deuteronomy 5:9. The most significant verses though are Exodus 34:6-7,

> Then the LORD passed in front of Moses and called out: "The LORD, the LORD God, is compassionate and gracious, slow to anger, abounding in loving devotion and faithfulness, maintaining loving devotion to a thousand generations, forgiving iniquity, transgression, and sin. Yet He will by no means leave the guilty unpunished; He will visit the iniquity of

the fathers on their children and grandchildren to the third and fourth generations."

This is clearly the scripture or a variation thereof that led the people to ask, "*who sinned this man or **his parents***," in John 9:2 concerning the man that was born blind. The people asking this question were referring to the tie between sin and sickness. This was asked several other places in the New Testament revealing how this scripture was taken. What God states here is that the result of sin which is death and which leads to sickness and disease, the predecessors of death, will be visited on the children and grandchildren. Genes are imprinted by family characteristics. Some of these characteristics are good. Some are not.

The question has been highly debated with regards to genetic determinism and the idea of choice between right or wrong. Some Christians have a difficult time aligning these aspects of science and faith. I see no problem with this nor with the fact that the Bible states in Deuteronomy 5:9 that God visits the iniquity of the fathers on their children to the third and fourth generation and then in Deuteronomy 24:16 (YHWH stated the same to Ezekiel in Ezekiel 18:20),

> Parents are not to be put to death for their children, nor children put to death for their parents; each will die for their own sin.

Why not, huh? Sounds quite dichotomous, doesn't it? Psalm 58:3 states that, *"Even from birth the wicked go astray; from the womb they are wayward, spreading lies."*

Scientifically and biblically, it is apparent to me that genetics have an impact on our sin nature. How can that be rectified with our freedom of choice? The Bible states that all have sinned. That we all were God's enemies. There are various genetic characteristics imprinted in us by the actions of unbelieving or unrepentant parents and to be more direct, fathers. Those sins will be "visited" upon us. In other words, we will have to deal with them. What does one do with a visitor? One either receives the visitor or sends the visitor on his way. It is your home. Your body. Your life. If you receive that iniquity, it will take up residence in your life just as it did your father's, but if you, by an act of your will, reject the visitor, it will not take up residence with you and it will not be your iniquity or sin. That is why both scriptures can be true. Why we both can experience the visitation of the sins of our fathers and at the same time reject them. If you accept it, be it alcoholism, drug addiction, adultery, thievery, or homosexuality, for example, then it becomes your sin. You might want to say that you have no choice, that you were born that way, as is today's custom. Indeed, you were. But it does not become yours until you accept it. At that point you are dealing with your own sin, not your father's. Thus, it is not difficult to settle the apparent dichotomy. Is there a genetic proclivity to various types of sin? Of course, there is. We can see it with our own eyes all around us. Does that alleviate any responsibility that we might have to address it? No, absolutely not. All have sinned, but we have a savior. You will not be punished for your father's sin, but if you make your father's sin your own, then you will most definitely pay for it. Unless you repent and receive Christ who has broken that curse. He set us all free, if we receive it that freedom will become our freedom.

What then does this have to do with disease? There are scientific and biblical connections between sin and sickness. Based on the statements in the New Testament, some will reject this and disavow what is clear in the Old Testament, but if they do, then they selectively read the New Testament. In John 5:14, Jesus stated when talking to the blind man,

> Later Jesus found him at the temple and said to him, "See, you are well again. Stop sinning or something worse may happen to you."

He said, "*You are well again*" and then He told the man, "*Stop sinning or something worse may happen to you.*"

To the paralytic in Mark 2:5, what did He tell him first off? Wasn't it, "*Son, your sins are forgiven?*" Jesus then healed the paralytic. For as He told the Pharisees, He had the power to do both. But He did not distinguish in this case, as He did in some others, between the man's sin and his disease. As stated in Proverbs 28:13,

> Whoever conceals their sins does not prosper, but the one who confesses and renounces them finds mercy.

It is known that many of today's diseases have genetic origins, just as our behavior does. As a genetic behavioral imprint can lead to sin, a genetic imprint relative to a disease can lead to sickness. These both come from the fall of man and from the pit of Hell itself. Just as sin can be traced in our genes, so can sickness and disease. It is not only scientific. It is biblical. Jesus alone delivered us and set us free from both – sin and sickness. For as it says in 1 Peter 2:24,

> "He himself bore our sins" in His body on the cross, so that we might die to sins and live for righteousness; "by His wounds you have been healed."

Six, most Believers don't have a true grasp on what impact their words have on their lives and on the lives of others. It is this aspect of our lives that drives sickness and disease in some people's lives. What needs to be grasped by most Believers is that God "spoke" the heavens and the Earth into existence. Remember He said, "Let there be," and there was. The God kind of faith is described in Romans 4:17b, as *"calling things that are not as though they were."*

Our words are so important to God that Jesus states in Matthew 12:36, that on the day of judgment we will give account for every "idle" or "careless" word which we have spoken. Proverbs 18:21 states,

> Death and life are in the power of the tongue: and they that love it shall eat the fruit thereof.

People take many of these scriptures to mean that the words that you say can have a positive or negative influence on your lives and the lives of others. This is most assuredly true. But there is a deeper truth here. Remember that every "idle" or "careless" word will be judged.

When you speak of sickness or disease how do you speak of it? Do you take ownership of it? Do you proclaim it to be your cold, your flu, or your cancer? Do you, with every ache or pain, proclaim some type of illness over yourself or do you battle what you feel with God's Word? James 3:6 states,

> The tongue also is a fire, a world of evil among the parts of the body. It corrupts the whole body, sets the whole course of one's life on fire, and is itself set on fire by Hell.

It states that the tongue corrupts, defiles, or pollutes the entire body. It does not say that the tongue corrupts the soul or spirit here, but rather, the "entire body." The corruption, defilement, or pollution of the body means that the body will degrade. Just as sickness and disease cause our bodies to do. Don't talk yourself into being sick. Clean up your words and enjoy life. Don't invite death and sickness to rule in your body. If you feel bad, then you feel bad. But rather state that you, "feel bad." Don't say, "I am sick," the first chance that you feel a little achy or have a headache.

I have battled cancer and was told that I had just a short time (months) to live years ago. Well-meaning people would ask me, how "my cancer was." My response was always that the cancer was not "mine" and that it came from the pit of Hell and belonged to Satan himself. This offended some people. But when you are standing on God's Word fighting for your health and your very life, that is not much of a concern. I was not intentionally trying to offend them. But neither was I going to speak what I knew to be contrary to God's Word just to avoid offending them, with my life hanging in the balance. I chose the fruit of life and still do today.

Seven, we can find ourselves and others that are close to us cursed by the words of others, intentionally and unintentionally. When I say a "curse" do not misunderstand it as saying something mean or offensive to someone. Words that are considered "curse" or "cuss" words in our culture and society, originated from the pit of Hell and that is why those words carry so much more weight than other words that mean the exact same things. You can easily think of a number of examples of what I am saying here. There are some words that are more scientifically or socially acceptable for an action, and then there are words that are considered cursing. Why? I believe the answer is the type or origin of the word in question in almost every circumstance.

Uttering those types of words is not what I am referring to here. I am speaking of the Greek word *katara* which, literally translated, means "an intensive hex." Yes, I am talking about intentional or unintentional witchcraft or sorcery. That is exactly what you do, when you speak a curse against someone or their family. I return again to the power of your words. Intentional curses carry the dark power of the demonic realm with them. That is why it states in Proverbs 26:2,

Like a fluttering sparrow or a darting swallow, an undeserved curse will not land on its intended victim.

Note that there are numerous locations in both the Old and New Testaments where curses and the relevance of them are discussed. In other words, as Believers there should be no instance that a curse comes to us and can land upon us. For it states in Galatians 3:13,

Christ redeemed us from the curse of the law by becoming a curse for us, for it is written: "Cursed is everyone who is hung on a pole."

We are redeemed from the curse of the law and thus from all curses unless, of course, we invite them into our homes, families, jobs, and lives. How would I do that, you may ask? A few examples would be:

1. By not obeying God's Word. God mentions in numerous places in the Word about the treatment of the poor, widows, and orphans. Treating them in ways that are not in line with the Word of God and His commands, opens you up to cursing, if they call out to God against you. Always make sure to treat all people fairly, but especially the poor, widowed, and orphaned. Also, in 1 Corinthians 5:5, the apostle Paul told the church at Corinth to turn the man who had taken his father's wife for his own "over to Satan for the destruction of the flesh." As individual believers and the church (corporate Body of Christ) walk in obedience to Him.

2. By bringing in and keeping objects that have demonic attachments. There are objects that represent demonic gods or idols that people bring into their homes and utilize them as art. Then there are items to which demons have attached themselves. Keeping these items in one's home or in what one calls "their possessions" can open the owner and his family up to many different demonic curses including sickness and disease. If you have any doubt about an object, remove it from your home. The Holy Spirit will give you guidance. Just ask Him.

3. By cursing others. The Golden Rule, which is found in Matthew 7:12, directs us, "to do unto others as we would have them do unto us." If you curse others, why would you not expect them to curse you? The Law of Sowing and Reaping states as much. Don't open the door to others cursing you, by you cursing them. Watch what you say about others.

4. Through unforgiveness. It is very clear in the Bible, that if you don't forgive others, then God is not able to forgive you. Your negative action blocks the way to receive His positive action. In Matthew 18, in the Parable of the Unforgiving Servant, the servant's master turned him over to the torturers, or as is stated in Matthew 18:34,

In anger his master handed him over to the jailers to be tortured, until he should pay back all he owed.

As stated in Luke 6:37,

> Do not judge, and you will not be judged. Do not condemn, and you will not be condemned. Forgive, and you will be forgiven.

CHAPTER THREE

WHY DON'T PEOPLE GET HEALED?

O ne, their focus is more on the symptoms, then on God's Word. We all want to feel better. I know that I do. I have told many people that I have felt bad, and I have felt good, and I would always choose to feel good. God has used sickness in my life to instruct, discipline, and mold me. That does not mean that He has made me sick, ordained me to be sick, caused me to be sick, or in any way, shape, or form willed sickness upon me. Sickness is from the pit of Hell. There is no sickness in Heaven and there certainly will be none in New Jerusalem. But we know that Romans 8:28 states:

And we know that all things work together for good to those who love God, to those who are the called according to His purpose...

This includes sickness and disease which are "things."

Hebrews 4:16 encourages us to approach God's throne with confidence,

Let us then approach the throne of grace with confidence, so that we may receive mercy and find grace to help us in our time of need.

Be it an athlete, writer, performer, mother, or any other role that we may fill in our day-to-day lives, those who succeed are most often those who have confidence. Those who think that they can. Those that have faith. It is not enough just to have faith, but rather we must have faith in God our Creator, Savior, King, and Lord and the truth of His Word.

Some of you will argue that your symptoms are real. I agree with you. As someone that has had some serious bouts with sickness and disease agrees. What I do not agree with you about is that those symptoms are more powerful and real than God's Holy Word. As Romans 3:4a states, "yea, let God be true, but every man a liar."

I don't care what your or my experience is and what it does or does not feel like. God's Word is true and until you grasp that singular principle you will struggle with health issues and grabbing hold of your healing.

Two, they run immediately to Google or some other search engine or their doctor the moment that any issue arises. "Well don't you believe in doctors and medical knowledge?" you may ask. I have a few doctors that tend to me that I have regular appointments with. Internal and external medical knowledge is the mercy of God in action. The doctors use their knowledge of physical maladies to drive out or control diseases and sicknesses. There is nothing wrong with this. It is like I tell people who tell me that God has made them sick and is teaching them something. I tell them not to go to the doctor then. That if they truly believe that God has made them sick, they would be fighting God to try to get the doctor to heal them. I believe that sickness and disease are both from Hell and, therefore, I have no problems with going to the doctor or hospital, if I need to.

It is easily seen where our faith lies when we get ill. It lies in the first thing that we turn to. If that is God in prayer, then it is God that you believe is the Great Physician. He can and will use anything to get you well that is usable, but where do you put your trust? Do you plug in healing scriptures and listen to them to build your faith, or do you immediately jump on Google or set an appointment with your doctor? Again, I state, I am not a Christian Scientist. There is nothing wrong with doing any of those things. But it is very evident that God and His Word are not where you put your primary trust and, until you do, you will have a difficult time battling sickness and disease. As stated in Psalm 118:8, "It is better to trust in the LORD than to put confidence in man."

Third, you disobey the physical requirements of your body. The body was created by God to be very adaptive and it is. But it can only go approximately three days without water, 30-40 days without food, and the record for going without sleep is just over 18 days. In other words, as adaptive as it is, it does have limits. The body also has a nutrient, chemical, and mineral balance all its own. It is 60% salt water with chlorine, bromine, iodine, etc. combining with sodium, potassium, calcium, magnesium, etc. to form the salts in the body. For instance, a change in the level of potassium in the body can have severe short-term and long-term impacts. This is true for the other substances that are a part of our make-up as well. So, in short, the way in which you eat can make it either more or less difficult for you to get healed.

The body speaks to us utilizing taste, touch, cravings, etc. to inform us as to what we need to consume to maintain its health. If you need water, you get thirsty. If you need salt, you desire to eat something salty. If you need carbs, you will crave quick energy drinks or starchy foods. It is very simple, but not so simple to many. If you grow deaf to your body, you will suffer health effects, just as if you have grown deaf to God's Spirit, you will suffer spiritual impacts. When my body is tired, it says rest. When it is thirsty, it says drink. When it is hungry, it says eat. But many override those natural cravings through the use or overuse of drugs (not necessarily illegal, say, for example, caffeine). The story is told of Yogi Berra and how when he was catching for the New York Yankees, he came down with what resembled arthritis, at its best, and paralysis, at its worst, in his hands and fingers. For a baseball player, this was career threatening. After the doctors finished research, it was finally determined that the tannic acid and caffeine in the gallon or so of tea that he drank daily was acting to create the malady. After he cut back drinking the tea, he fully recovered and went on to a Hall of Fame career. Our bodies will tell us when it is getting too much of what we are giving it if we will just listen.

Fourth, people build the basis for their faith in healing from personal experiences, experiences someone else shares with them, or some preaching that they heard from some great teacher of faith. Their house is built on the sand and when the enemy attacks they have no true foundation of faith for physical healing. People get highly insulted if you suggest that they don't really believe in healing. The truth is that your faith in God's desire and ability to heal must be from God's Word, the Bible. No set of experiences or sermons is a firm foundation for your faith. Shared experiences can give people hope that God will move, but it does not give them faith. For every good experience there is a bad experience. For every positive sermon there is a sermon that says that healing is not for today. If you try to build your faith on those items, then you will find yourself like the man in James 1 who finds himself tossed to and fro by the wind and waves of doubt and receives nothing from the Lord. Why does he receive nothing? Simply because he has no or little faith. How many times have you heard someone say something to the effect of, "I just don't understand why God did not heal that person? She was the kindest and most loving saint I have ever known." God moves based on your faith. God can move mercifully and miraculously to heal. He is sovereign. That is His choice. But that is apparently not the preferred method of healing as shown by Jesus in the Gospels.

Believers confuse love, hope, kindness, etc. as reasons that God will move on their or someone else's behalf and heal them. The Bible says simply in Hebrews 6:11,

And without faith it is impossible to please God because anyone who comes to Him must believe that He exists and that He rewards those who earnestly seek him.

Jesus always had the person make a declaration of their faith in Him before performing the needed healing, as did the apostles. In Acts 14:9, it states,

> He listened to Paul as he was speaking. Paul looked directly at him and saw that he had faith to be healed....

Not that Paul saw that he looked like a nice guy or that he was well-respected within the community, but rather that "he had faith." "Okay," you say, "how am I supposed to obtain that faith you speak of?" Glad you asked. Again, I turn to God's Word which is the only sure source of truth which states in Romans 10:17, "So *then faith comes by hearing, and hearing by the word of God.*" So, according to God's Word, faith comes by hearing God's Word. It comes by hearing it not once, twice, or three times, but as stated in Isaiah 28:9-10,

> Whom will He teach knowledge? And whom will He make to understand the message? Those just weaned from milk? Those just drawn from the breasts? For precept must be upon precept, precept upon precept, Line upon line, line upon line, Here a little, there a little.

No, it is not reading something once or twice, but as stated here, it is by consistent study over a long period of time.

Also, remember the Parable of the Sower in Mark 4:3-8 and then in Mark 4:13, where after being asked by the disciples to explain the parable, Jesus stated,

> Then Jesus said to them, "Do you not understand this parable? Then how will you understand any of the parables?"

As you will recollect, this parable is about faith. That is why Jesus states that without understanding the Parable of the Sower, they would not understand any of the other parables. It is about the seeds of faith sown in the hearts of people and what the enemy does to try to keep those seeds from growing and producing fruit. Some of it is pecked out by demonic birds (Did God really say that?); some is sown on rocky ground where the person "hears the word once with joy" but there is no root and at the first sign of trouble or persecution they fall away; some falls among thorns, which represent the things of this life, be they bad (worries) or good (riches) or neither (desires) and these things choke out the Word (experience overcomes truth); yet some find good soil, grow, and produce good fruit. This represents the life of faith. Consistently plant, for you do not know when you will receive a harvest . As Galatians 6:9 states, "Let us not become weary in doing good, for at the proper time we will reap a harvest if we do not give up."

When you plant seeds, you do so with your eye toward receiving a harvest. But you don't plant corn seeds and expect to harvest peas or plant pecans and expect that tree to give you peaches. Like produces like and the same is true in the Kingdom of God. If you want healing, plant healing seed; if you want wisdom, plant wisdom seed; if you want to see someone receive Christ, give them salvation seed; etc. See what I am saying? I battle various physical maladies. The enemy is, at times, relentless. I listen to healing scriptures by John Hagee every night before I go to bed. Now those are not the only scriptures I listen to or study, but since I have this issue that I deal with, I put quite a few of those seeds in the soil of my heart. You should do the same.

The fifth reason that people don't get healed is because they hold grudges and/or maintain a root of bitterness in their lives. They walk in unforgiveness toward others. "What does unforgiveness have to do with our physical healing?" you might ask. There are many scriptures and, as far as that goes, psychological texts that deal with the impact of unforgiveness and bitterness on our daily lives, including our health. The most revealing, though, can be found in Matthew 18:21-35 in a parable which is called "the Parable of the Unmerciful Servant." Matthew 18:21-35 *states,*

> Then Peter came to Jesus and asked, "Lord, how many times shall I forgive my brother who sins against me? Up to seven times?" Jesus answered, "I tell you, not just seven times, but seventy-seven times! Because of this, the kingdom of Heaven is like a king who wanted to settle accounts with his servants. As he began the settlements, a debtor was

brought to him owing ten thousand talents. Since the man was unable to pay, the master ordered that he be sold to pay his debt, along with his wife and children and everything he owned. Then the servant fell on his knees before him. 'Have patience with me,' he begged, 'and I will pay back everything.' His master had compassion on him, forgave his debt, and released him. But when that servant went out, he found one of his fellow servants who owed him a hundred denarii. He grabbed him and began to choke him, saying, 'Pay back what you owe me!' So, his fellow servant fell down and begged him, 'Have patience with me, and I will pay you back.' But he refused. Instead, he went and had the man thrown into prison until he could pay his debt. When his fellow servants saw what had happened, they were greatly distressed, and they went and recounted all of this to their master. Then the master summoned him and declared, 'You wicked servant! I forgave all your debt because you begged me. Shouldn't you have had mercy on your fellow servant, just as I had on you?' In anger his master turned him over to the jailers to be tortured, until he should repay all that he owed. That is how My Heavenly Father will treat each of you unless you forgive your brother from your heart."

This begins because Peter apparently had been having to deal with someone who was constantly offending him in some manner. With some of the old fisherman habits coming out of Peter, he obviously was looking for when he might have clearance from Jesus to go ring the guy's bell. So, he is trying to get some guidance on how often he needs to forgive this guy. I am sure Peter felt quite magnanimous when he suggested seven times. Jesus counters with 490 times. I am sure that Jesus' response staggered Peter and does so to many of us today. Now you should not allow anyone to sin against you 490 times. Forgive them but make an effort to remove yourself from their influence and thus remove yourself from harm's way. But what Jesus is getting at is that the enemy, Satan, is going to bring that sin against you and to your mind repeatedly. That is where the 490 times comes from. You will feel the pain of the offense each time as though it had just happened. So, what should you do in this situation to keep from carrying unforgiveness in your heart? I personally intentionally pray a blessing on that person every time Satan brings it to mind. Remember, "we war not against flesh and blood." It is Satan's intent to keep you both bound up by this offense. If the demons involved have to deal with you praying a blessing on the person every time they bring it to your mind, trust me, they will quit. This is against their orders and intent, and it also prevents them from getting fed the negative spiritual energy that keeps them going.

To clarify to Peter, and the rest of the disciples, the true importance of forgiveness and why they should forgive, Jesus shared the parable. Within the parable, someone who is owed very much (us all) is forgiven magnanimously without condition or question. Then that same person goes out and refuses forgiveness to one who owes him little. The Master (God), is, of course, angered at the injustice of the circumstance and the unfairness of the one that withheld forgiveness. The one that withholds forgiveness is then handed over to "the torturers." The Greek word for "torturer" used here is *basanistes* which means "one who elicits truth by means of the rack." "The rack" was later considered the most painful means of medieval torture. Pain and agony can be mental and emotional and can be excruciating. But what is pictured in this parable as being administered is a physical torture. Obviously, the torturers that Jesus was referring to were likely demonic in nature. They would enjoy taking out their sadistic imaginations on men and women that had withheld forgiveness and thus, by doing so, had opened themselves to physical attack.

How long would it take to pay all that you owed? Forever. The only respite would be for you to repent and forgive the one that sinned against you. Jesus states as much in the final verse of the parable. Not only would you have no basis to ask for healing which came through the forgiveness granted through Christ at Calvary, but you would open yourself up to other sickness and disease (physical, mental, and emotional) to be inflicted upon you by "the tormentors." As stated by the Apostle Paul in Romans 12:17-21, pursue the following course of action,

> Do not repay anyone evil for evil. Carefully consider what is right in the eyes of everybody. If it is possible on your part, live at peace with everyone. Do not avenge yourselves, beloved, but leave room for God's wrath. For it is written: "Vengeance is Mine; I will repay, says the Lord." On the contrary, "If your enemy is hungry, feed him; if he is thirsty, give him a drink. For in so doing, you will heap burning coals

on his head." Do not be overcome by evil but overcome evil with good.

Paul had been slandered, abused, beaten, stoned until dead, jailed, shipwrecked, and attacked by Believers and unbelievers alike. He had every reason to be bitter, but instead he responded as dictated in Romans. If we too would act in forgiveness, bitterness will not hinder our physical, mental, or emotional healing.

Another reason (sixth) that people don't get well is that they choose not to. They desire to remain sick for any number of reasons. Personally, I, as I have shared with my friends and children many times, have found that I would always rather be and feel well than to feel and be sick, diseased, or injured. But some people are not that way. We have all known them. They get so much attention from being sick or not being whole in some way that they subconsciously or some consciously choose to remain that way.

When this is taken to the extreme it is called Munchausen's Syndrome which is identified as a psychological/psychiatric disorder. Another similar disorder is Factitious Disorder. I know some of you will not agree, but I believe that in many situations in which we call things psychological disorders, those things are actually demonically induced. The demon or disorder may have found an entry due to a traumatic instance or group of instances in a person's life. Mental health professionals call Factitious Disorder a "disorder of deception." As a Believer you will recognize the one who is known as the "great deceiver" in the Bible, Satan himself. I do not recall anywhere in scripture where Jesus ever counseled those who came to him. He did, however, give them advice or instructions before he either healed them or cast out a demonic presence. Don't misunderstand. I am not against psychological or even psychiatric treatment (for instance for schizophrenia or being bipolar). If something helps you, then you are to be judged on how you deal with that sickness or disease. I take pain medication for intermittent pain. I am still trusting God for complete deliverance, but until that time comes, I, as stated herein, am inclined to take some medical assistance to not be in pain. Most of us would and do the same.

On the other hand, if we don't face the fact that most of these sicknesses or diseases, whether physical or emotional, are from the pit of Hell, then we will never in this life overcome them completely. Mark Brazee, author of 365 *Days of Healing*, tells the story of three people of whom he knew that had diabetes that were on mission trips with him. One of them stated that they were trusting God for their healing and threw away their insulin. A few days later this person went into diabetic shock and almost died. The other two people continued to take their medication and would state every time they took it, "Thank you God for healing my body by Jesus stripes." Within a few months these two Believers were absolutely healed and no longer needed their insulin. There is nothing spiritual about not taking medication. There is something spiritual about believing for the Great Physician to heal us.

Some people, from the very young to the very old, will choose sickness over health just for the sake of the attention and sympathy they might get. They become so obsessed with being the center of that attention and so concerned that, if they are well, they will not be the center of attention that they not only refuse any medication that might help them, but they also reject any prayer or the Word of God itself about being healed. This is a spiritual stronghold, and it must be broken. The unclean spirit (demon) that is in control of that person must be taken control of and commanded to leave in the Name of Jesus. Being able to do this though, requires someone close to the person who is willing and able to confront him or her about it and show him or her the truth in God's Word. All the people in the Body of Christ can pray according to God's Word and in great faith, but if the person does not change his or her mindset (to be delivered from the stronghold), they will not ever be healed.

Finally, the last reason (seventh) that I will touch upon, is the fact that some Believers will only accept the miraculous. If the healing does not come in the form of an instantaneous miracle, which happens immediately, right then and there, that person will not fight the good fight of faith. There are many ways that the Bible sets forth for us to be healed. At this point in my walk with God, I have difficulty understanding Believers who do not believe that God wants them and, for that matter, all of His children healed and walking in divine health. The fact that we all aren't healed does not point to His stated desire now any more than it did when Jesus was questioned by the leper in Matthew 8:2-3,

> A man with leprosy came and knelt before him and said, "Lord, if you are willing, you can make me clean." Jesus reached out His hand and touched the man. "I am willing," He said. "Be clean!" Immediately he was cleansed of his leprosy.

I will discuss this more later. But I challenge you to show me anywhere in the Gospels that Jesus did not heal "all who came to Him" unless it was due to their own lack of faith.

That being said, it is not the fact that with some they don't believe that God wants to heal them, but it is that they will not receive anything short of a miracle. I mean, even the gifts of the Spirit listed in 1 Corinthians 12 include the gift of faith, the gift of healing, and the gift of working miracles. This differentiates among these gifts, thus meaning that the Spirit moves in a different way concerning each of them. As we all know, the body was created to heal itself. It is only due to the "penalty of death, sickness, and disease" visited upon us because of the fall that we experience sickness at all.

A miracle obviously does not have to be one of healing, but it can be. Neither does increased faith to believe for something necessarily have to do with healing either, but it can. Healing on the other hand quite obviously has to do with healing as stated in the name of the gift itself. Actually, none of these gifts give any indication as to the timing associated with them for any of them to occur. They can be instantaneous or occur over a period of time. We humans obviously prefer something that happens immediately. The sensational occurrences are what bring the Body of Christ to their feet. If a person is healed over a long period of time, it is not nearly as sensational and, many feel, not nearly as spiritual. As for myself, speaking as one who has walked out of a diagnosis of stage four metastatic prostate cancer (with a few months to live or so I was told) over a period of time, can tell you, that while I would have preferred the immediate more sensational deliverance than what I have gone through, my faith has been strengthened in a much greater way than a miraculous immediate deliverance ever could have. I have had to fight the good fight. I have walked closely with my Savior and friend Jesus, up until now, in a manner that I have never known Him. As my wife will attest, my God and I have had some very real discussions. Some very heated discussions. It is called a relationship and it is what God created us for. Oh yes, I still fight the good fight . . . but I have been fighting that good fight for quite a few years now. Not bad for a man whom the doctor told not to ride his bicycle because a fall may totally cripple him for life. I have ridden my bike a few thousand miles since then and have taken some pretty serious falls. No broken bones. For as stated in Psalm 34:19-20,

> The righteous person may have many troubles, but the Lord delivers him from them all; he protects all of his bones, not one of them will be broken.

The fighting of this fight is not easy, so some choose not to fight it. Some go home to be with Jesus and there is nothing wrong with that. What is wrong is when we blame God for being more inclined to heal one over the other. As is clearly stated in Romans 2:11, "*For God does not show favoritism.*" If you choose not to come to Him for healing or if you get to the point of choice and you choose to go home, then there is no condemnation in Christ. But dare not put the blame on God for whatever reason that you do not receive that healing. I have been to the place where it would be easy to choose to go home. The fact that I am still here is to God's glory and not due to my great faith. I grow in faith, as we all can and do; as we fight the fight of faith in whatever area we struggle in our lives. Know that He has granted us His gifts, our faith, agreement of the others in the Body of Christ, and the leaders of the local bodies to pray over us. We are not alone. Fight the good fight. "To live is Christ, to die is gain." Paul chose to live on. We are in a day that He needs mighty warriors. This is a war for the hearts and souls of men and women everywhere. Miracles are nice but fight the good fight. Your faith will grow, and you will be able to touch the lives of others.

CHAPTER FOUR

HOW DO I RECEIVE HEALING?

How do I receive my healing? What do I do to put myself in the best possible position to be healed? I will touch on numerous ways in which the Word of God sets out for us to be healed. If the Word doesn't state it, then one shouldn't spend any time or effort invested in that means of healing. If it does, ignore all faith killers that would argue against it based upon their experience, theology, etc., and let Romans 3:4a prevail and *"Let God be true and every man a liar."* One must come to the point in his or her study of the Word that, no matter how venerated and well-spoken some theologians and preachers are, that means nothing if what they teach is contrary to God's Word. They can twist the scripture and manipulate it until the End of Days, but that does not change God's written Word – the Bible. And as Alistair Begg stated, *"The main things are the plain things, and the plain things are the main things."* You can place some pastors and theologians in the category of those spoken of in Romans 1:22, "Although they claimed to be wise, they became fools." It is a shame that there are those who have denied healing to those that adhere to their teaching. That being said, let's focus on the positive ways God has presented to heal us knowing that as stated in Acts 10:38, Jesus healed "all" who were oppressed by the devil. The Greek translation of the word "all" is the word *pas* which much to my surprise means, "each, every, or all."

First, let's investigate Jesus' ministry and notice how most of the people were healed. Every time Jesus healed someone they were healed by faith. If you don't believe it, all you have to do is take the Gospels and read every account of Jesus healing someone. If that is the case then, just as is the case for being born again, we would receive our healing in the same manner. As noted in Ephesians 2:8, *"For it is by grace you have been saved through faith, and this not from yourselves; it is the gift of God."* The word "saved" is from the Greek word *sozo*. One of its root meanings is, "to heal." It doesn't state, to heal spiritually, emotionally, mentally, or physically alone, but simply, "to heal." Some pastors try to spiritualize the meaning of the word and make it only refer to a spiritual meaning. There is nothing in the scripture that would indicate that to be the case.

So, how do I get the faith to be healed? Well, the same way in which you get faith for anything else. As stated in God's

Word in Romans 10:17, "So *then faith comes by hearing, and hearing by the word of God.*" This is clarified in the Parable of the Sower as shared by Jesus in Mark Chapter 4. In the Parable of the Sower, it is clear that the Word of God is equivalent to seed being sown, as is succinctly stated in Mark 4:14. As Jesus explained the parable, there were different outcomes for the different types of soil the seed fell upon. The best outcome was that the seed fell on good soil and bore much fruit from the seed. Jesus stated in Mark 4:13, "*Do you not understand this parable? Then how will you understand any of the parables?*"

What did He mean by these questions? Why wouldn't they understand any of the parables? Because the parables were based on the Word of God being sown and the seed finding good soil. If it did not, faith which comes by hearing, and hearing by the Word of God would not come. Also note, that if you are a farmer and want wheat, what do you plant? Wheat seed. Correct. If you want corn, plant corn. Peas, plant peas. The same tenet applies to the seed sown into our hearts. If you need peace, read and study scriptures on peace, not on prosperity. If you need healing, read and study scripture based on healing, not on being free from addiction. Plant the seed that you need a crop from. It is a simple concept, but one not fully understood by many pastors and teachers. Also, remember that crops grow over time. Every healing is not miraculous (or immediate). We all love the miraculous but being healed, whether miraculously or over time, is just that, being healed. Reality is, that truth be told, it is probably better for most people that they receive their healing over a period of time. One reason being that it gives the person time to spend in the Word and with the Word-giver (God). Also, people, when healed miraculously, who don't have a base from God's Word in healing, can see their healing being stolen from them by the enemy. Once again, I urge you to look closely at the different outcomes in the Parable of the Sower. There are many tools to use. Obviously, study all of God's Word on healing. Listen to healing scripture while awake and as you go to sleep. Fill your spirit with God's Word.

Second, as we all know, not all Believers are strong enough in God's Word or mature enough to receive in the manner mentioned. Over time, they should grow to that point but, by that time, they could be dead. Also, as stated in God's Word in Leviticus 26:8, "*Five of you will chase a hundred, and a hundred of you will chase ten thousand, and your enemies will fall by the sword before you.*" This is stated concerning the nation of Israel battling human forces. But I believe this scripture has a spiritual meaning as well; that it also refers to battling demonic forces which is where sickness and disease come from. That being said, the second option that we will address from which we may receive our healing turns to those who should be the representatives of the faith in our churches – our elders. In James 5:14-15, the following is stated,

> Is anyone among you sick? Let them call the elders of the church to pray over them and anoint them with oil in the name of the Lord. And the prayer offered in faith will make the sick person well; the Lord will raise them up. If they have sinned, they will be forgiven.

What is being stated here is very straight forward. It is clear that if someone in the congregation is sick, for whatever reason, they are to call upon the elders or those who are mature in the faith and have been appointed and anointed by God to lead a specific congregation. That would simply mean that if I am a Believer and a member of a specific congregation, then I should approach the leadership of that congregation to anoint me with oil and pray for me in the Name of Jesus. The scripture states emphatically and very clearly that the prayer for healing, when offered in faith, will make the sick person well and that the Lord Jesus will "raise" that individual up. The word for "raise" is the same Greek word, *egeiro* used in Matthew 8:15, when stating that Peter's mother-in-law arose from her bed of sickness. Some folks like to say that the word, *egeiro*, here refers to us being raised up at the last day (which I believe to refer to the *harpazo* or catching away). This to me, is, once again, a misdirected effort to create a gospel where one's personal experiences have similar weight to God's Word. Pure and simple, our experiences do not. When your experience departs from coinciding with the Word of God, then your experience becomes of secondary importance. As stated in John 17:17b, "*His Word is truth.*" If your experience does not line up with the Word, then search the scriptures as to why. This scripture goes on to state that even if this sickness had been caused by sin that the sin would be forgiven.

As always, there will be those who continually want to twist God's Word to line up with their own interpretation thereof. This has been the case ever since the Word of God was first preached. I am not so foolish as to believe that every interpretation of scripture that I hold is perfect. Many of my own personal interpretations have changed over the years, as I have studied to show myself approved, and the Spirit of God has given me further and deeper revelation. If you have not experienced that, then you should question whether you are a disciple of a pharisee, hardened by your own theological beliefs to the point of excluding the beliefs of others, without even so much as bothering to question your own personal beliefs. Just because that is the religious background in which you grew up or that it is what you have studied in seminary or Bible College, that does not necessarily make it true. A lie once taught is evermore a lie, no matter how many more times it be taught. A lie taught for hundreds or even thousands of years does not lend more veracity to whatever lie is taught. As stated in Romans 3:4a. "*Let God be true and every man a liar.*"

A third way in which to be healed, is clearly stated in James 5:16,

> Therefore, confess your sins to each other and pray
> for each other so that you may be healed. The prayer
> of a righteous man has great power to prevail.

Now as stated in James 5:14-15, for the very physically and/or spiritually weak, the elders of the church should pray. But, as is clearly stated in James 5:16, we do not need to allow ourselves to get to the point where we need to call for the elders. We, as members of the body, can "*confess our sins to each other and pray for each other that we may be healed.*" Note that the word, "heal" here is the root of the Greek word *iaomai,* which typically means "to physically be healed." It is not as broad-based as *sozo*, which, as previously shown, refers to complete physical and spiritual healing. The last line of verse 16 alludes to the fact that even one righteous man can accomplish much. The person does not have to be an elder to pray for others and see them delivered, but merely a person of faith that prays fervently and effectively. So, not only can you get the elders of the church to pray for you, you can also ask a righteous brother or sister to pray for your healing so you may be physically healed after confessing your sin to another which would, in this case, be that same brother or sister.

By implication, it is clear that the prayer and anointing by the elders of the church is a special anointing with regard to deliverance. For the person can be completely delivered by prayer. No matter what the root cause of the sickness is, whether it be rooted in the physical, the spiritual or in a demonic warfare, or a spiritual imprisonment, this type of prayer frees us. But, if the cause is sin, repent and a righteous servant of the Most High God can pray you back to health.

A fourth biblical method from which we might receive healing is in the same way that we might receive anything from God. That is, for us to pray in faith for it. As it states clearly in Matthew 21:22: "*And all things, as many as you might ask in prayer, believing, you will receive.*" This is clearly stated. Again, "the main things are plain." There are some who will carry on about context, etc., in an attempt to disprove or at least dilute the meaning of scriptures, such as these. Does this scripture include healing? Well, let's see, the Greek word for "all" in this scripture means, well, let's see, it means, "all!" Some will counter, "Well, that can't be true, because I prayed for so and so and she did not receive healing." Well, let's see again. Oh yeah, the scripture also states, *"ask in prayer, believing."* Apparently, you weren't believing or, maybe you did not read all of Hebrews 6:12 which at the end states, *"be imitators of those who through faith and patience inherit the promises."* That's right! We all want an immediate answer to our prayers. I am with you. I am the same way. But I did not receive an immediate reprieve from drug addiction or from cancer. I had to be patient and allow God's Word to grow me in faith and in His Spirit to use that faith to deliver me and heal me.

I worked on the mission field, worked for Youth for Christ in the local high schools, and served as an elder in Word of God Church in Brownsville, Texas for several years. My Pastor there was Pastor Jerry Cooke. He and I would have chats from time to time. One time we were talking about God's faithfulness and Hebrews 6:12. Jerry looked at me and in his Texas twang said, "Bob, you know what? God is just like the cavalry. He always arrives right in the nick of time." He paused for a moment and then turned back to me and stated, "And you know what else? I, more often than not, turn to God and tell Him, 'Lord I appreciate that and all, but if it is all the same to you, I'll take mine now.'" I have never forgotten that. I, to this day, still share this not only with others, but with God Himself at many times when I am tired of waiting for an answer.

On the other hand, you might have misconstrued God's answer. Maybe just because God did not answer your prayer the way you dictated the answer to Him, you feel that you have not been answered. God will always answer prayers in your best interests. If He would have answered my prayers the way I have prayed them throughout my life, then I would be my own divine providence and He would just be my muscle, so to speak. I also would add that my life would be a mess instead of full of divine providence. That being said, I will also point out that God will never, ever, ever, deny His own Word. As I have stated a number of other times herein, Romans 3:4a states, "*Let God be true and every man a liar.*" Just because you have not received an answer to your prayer, don't try to make scripture conform to your experience. This is the devil's trap. At some point, you may possibly need to face the fact that you do not have sufficient faith to obtain what you prayed for. For, it states in Hebrews 11:6,

> And without faith it is impossible to please God because anyone who comes to him must believe that He exists and that He rewards those who earnestly seek him.

I guarantee you that if you try to tell someone who has been in church for years that they don't have sufficient faith, most will become very angry. That is why you see that, through the years, many have rather tried to conform God's Word to their experiences instead of seeking the truth, by getting into God's Word, so their faith can grow. How do you get faith again? As stated in Romans 10:17, faith comes from hearing God's Word. As covered previously, Jesus laid out the format for building faith in the Parable of the Sower.

Another thing which you can do, if your faith seems to not be sufficient to you, is to get others to pray in faith with you. If I try to lift 1,000 pounds on my own, I am never going to get it done. My strength (faith is merely spiritual strength) is insufficient. I can think that I am strong enough. I can speak to the weight, I can shout at it but, in the end, it still is going to be too heavy for me to lift. I could spend years working with weights and then maybe be able to lift the weight by myself or I could get nine of my strongest friends to help me lift the weight. Now that means that we are all just lifting 100 pounds each with our legs. Most people with even nominal strength can do that. We would have no problem in lifting that weight. The same is true when it comes to prayer. While my faith may not be sufficient to deal with a specific issue on its own, if I get several people of whom I know to operate at some level of faith, say concerning healing, then we should be able to address and deal with the issue without much effort on our parts together.

It states in Matthew 18:19,

> Again, truly I tell you that if two of you on earth agree about anything they ask for, it will be done for them by my Father in Heaven.

There are some who disagree that this scripture points to the fact that agreement in prayer helps to make that prayer stronger. In fact, I ask as many people as possible, those who can pray in faith, to agree with me in prayer when praying for anything. This is another scripture that some will say, "That is not what it says. That is out of context." Well, let's use a little logic here. If something is true, then all of it must be true. This, in fact, is how the enemy goes about deceiving many Believers. He will mix in a little lie with the whole statement.

That little lie, as Jesus stated, permeates the entire loaf of bread like yeast.

A lie within a statement does not remove or reduce the level of truth in that statement when it comes to statements of fact that can stand on their own. Even though it contradicts common sense, some will state that Matthew 18:19 must only be about church discipline because that is what Jesus is discussing at the time. The fact that faith can move a mountain does not just apply to the mountain. It applies to any other object that might need to be moved. Matthew 18:19 states, *"Again, truly I tell you that if two of you on earth agree about anything they ask for, it will be done for them by my Father in Heaven."*

Let's break that statement down. First, when Jesus wants to bring emphasis to a statement, He says, *"truly."* Note His statements in the Gospels and that much is plain to see. Next, we see who He is referring to. *"If two of you on earth."* That means, any two of us that occupy space on Earth. That means, to comply with the context, there must be two of us living on this Earth. Now what is He referring to? *"Agree about anything they ask for."* You know what the word "anything" means? Ah, the word, "all" comes up again. It covers, "all." It covers, "anything." Not just matters that are covered by church discipline, but "all" or "the whole." Is healing included in "all?" I think so. Is forgiveness included in "all?" Seems like it might be. Is a job request included? Yep, it is. Now let's see what happens when two agree about anything. *"It will be done for them by my Father in Heaven."* Done means to, "come into being," "come about," or "happen." I believe it is relatively clear that this statement, while being used in a discussion regarding church discipline, refers to a much broader base of items and issues... unless, "all" means something that I don't think it does.

A fifth way to receive healing is to focus on Jesus' substitution for your complete salvation. Everything that you can receive from God by faith is due to the substitutionary act of Jesus' giving His life for our life, for taking our sins and giving us His righteousness, for giving us His peace for our conflict, and, in accord with what I am discussing, substituting stripes on His back (wounds) for our sicknesses and diseases. Some still choose to refute this even though the scripture is quite clear that Christ indeed did act in this substitutionary manner. Even in the Old Testament, this is also made crystal clear, as stated in Isaiah 53:5,

> But He was pierced for our transgressions, He was crushed for our iniquities; the punishment that brought us peace was on Him, and by His wounds we are healed.

The Hebrew word for "wounds" is *chabburah* which refers to scourging with a whip, as Jesus was with the flagrum or flagellum (which is a lead tipped whip), thus you get stripes. Some people want to spiritualize this by saying that the reference to healing is spiritual. I would like those people to take a couple of strokes from a flagrum and then tell me how spiritual the strokes felt. The whipping was physical and the healing that is referred to is physical. The Hebrew word for "healed" in this passage is *rapha*, which clearly relates to a physical healing based upon its background.

This substitutionary act is again referenced in 1 Peter 2:24 after Jesus was reportedly flogged according to Pilate's orders in John 19:1. The New Testament reference is,

"He himself bore our sins" in His body on the cross, so that we might die to sins and live for righteousness; "by His wounds you have been healed."

Once again, the scripture, though clearly referring to a physical wound, is watered down by those wanting to spiritualize it to better line up with their theology. This argument is one which states that divine healing is not for today or is only for those who God determines by His will to heal.

I will once again point out that the word "wound" in the Greek is *molopes*, which literally is a bruise or stripe left on the body by scourging, an obvious physical act. The Greek word *iaomai*, which, according to Strong's Concordance, means "heal," generally of the physical, sometimes of spiritual, disease." Note the word was translated as being "heal, generally of the physical." That means that the primary translation of this word means, "physical healing." It could mean spiritual healing, and praise God, I believe that Christ Jesus healed us from our spiritual maladies as well as our physical maladies. But it quite clearly in the definition states, "generally physical" and includes all healing.

Why then, you may ask, do ministers and others in the Body of Christ deny the clear definition and meaning of those verses? Because it does not fit their experience or possibly their theology. There are those within the Body that seek to fit the Word of God into their experiences, as opposed to fitting their experiences into God's Word. What do I mean by that? Well, the problem that most people have with the scriptures that I have just quoted, is that they or someone whom they loved or knew well, did not receive their healing. Therefore they, in an attempt to fit God's Word into their experiences, water down what these scriptures say.

Mark Brazee shares an interesting response that the Holy Spirit gave him, when one of these "faith killers" stood up during a teaching on healing that he was giving and stated that Mark was wrong. He stated that it was clear that 1 Peter 2:24 referred only to spiritual healing. Mark then proceeded to ask him if he was born again. The gentleman responded, "Yes." Mark then asked the gentleman why he needed to be born again. He responded, "*Because I was spiritually dead.*" Mark then asked him, "What good would healing do for a dead spirit?" Of course, the man had no answer because healing is for the living not the dead. It was the man's spirit that received new life through Jesus' death and resurrection and His body that received healing through Jesus' stripes (scourging).

It is clear in these scriptures what is meant. These theologians, ministers, and lay people make the mistake of not believing that the same pattern that is used for salvation (being born again) is the very same pattern that God uses for healing. Let's address that issue. First, Jesus took our sins and our sicknesses and diseases. Second, we are saved by faith, and we are healed by faith. Third, not everyone is saved from sin and not everyone is healed from sickness and disease, and it is typically for the same reason. They don't apply their faith.

If you want someone to be saved, minister salvation scriptures. If you want them to be healed, minister healing scriptures. "So then faith comes by hearing and hearing by the Word of God," Romans 10:17. If you want peas, don't plant corn seed and expect peas, if you want corn don't plant radishes and expect corn, etc.

What you get in many churches, though, is the faith killing prayer, "God if it be your will, please heal so and so." If you don't know what God's will is then get in His Word until He shows you. It is not very hard to find out that God desires to heal you.

Jesus healed whom? All who came to Him. He had previously told the disciples that if they wanted to know the Father's will then watch Him and they would know the Father's will. One of the first people that Jesus healed was a leper and His response to the leper showed that He knew that this would be a question that people carried with them throughout this age (church). In Matthew 8:2-3, it states,

> A man with leprosy came and knelt before him and said, "Lord, if you are willing, you can make me clean." Jesus reached out His hand and touched the man. "I am willing," He said. "Be clean!" Immediately he was cleansed of his leprosy.

The leper asked Jesus if He was willing. Jesus responded, "I am willing." That has remained His response throughout history. So, if you want to be physically healed, focus on that scripture. For by His physical stripes, you were physically healed. That doesn't mean that it will be a miraculous healing every time. In fact, healing may take some time. It doesn't mean that all the symptoms will go away immediately. Your spirit first applies the faith for the healing and then the healing manifests itself. It can be a war. Don't give up. Keep fighting. Keep focusing on these scriptures. *"Faith comes by hearing and hearing by the Word of God." Romans 10:17.*

A sixth way to receive healing is by using the name of Jesus. The name above all names. The Apostle Paul wrote in Philippians 2:9,

> Therefore, God exalted him to the highest place and gave him the name that is above every name, that at the name of Jesus every knee should bow, in Heaven and on earth and under the earth, and every tongue acknowledges that Jesus Christ is Lord, to the glory of God the Father.

What exactly does this mean to you regarding healing? First off, everything is called by a name. Dogs, chemical compounds, insects, and diseases. It means that sickness and disease must bow their knee to the name of Jesus. That is exactly what Paul stated. Now again, you might want to attempt to spiritualize this scripture, because you don't fully believe it. As I have previously stated, that only hurts you, not me. So, have at it. The problem comes when you feel led to espouse your false belief to others. It puts them into the place of being double-minded. And as stated in James 1:6-8,

> But when you ask, you must believe and not doubt, because the one who doubts is like a wave of the sea, blown and tossed by the wind. That person should

not expect to receive anything from the Lord. Such a person is double-minded and unstable in all they do.

May God forgive us all for the times that our misinformed quotations of the Bible and misguided sharing of our own faithless experiences has hampered the faith of another and brought them to the same point at which we had originally found ourselves. That of receiving nothing from God.

As stated in Acts 4:12, "*Salvation is found in no one else, for there is no other name under Heaven given to mankind by which we must be saved.*" There is salvation for mankind in "*no other name,*" than the name of Jesus. For the sake of the reader, I will once again point out the meaning of the root Greek word *sozo* which in English translates as "saved." This is another scripture that at least one in every crowd is going to jump in and try to spiritualize and state that it only refers to being born again. I am sorry. That is not only not what it states. It actually states the absolute opposite, no matter what your seminary professor may have taught you or what your experience is. It is used to mean saved, healed, preserved, and rescued (delivered). The first word "salvation" or in Greek *soteria* is used to denote welfare, prosperity, deliverance, preservation, salvation, and safety. These are words that are inclusive of body, soul, and spirit. Again, if you choose to deny that through the name of Jesus you can be physically healed, then that is your choice and impacts no one, but you, and I have no problem with that. But when you feel the necessity to begin to spiritualize the term and teach others the same thing, then you are doing harm to many who will read what you wrote or hear what you stated, and it will bring doubt to their minds. If you want to "twist the scripture to your own destruction or loss" as stated in 1 Peter 3:16, that is your choice. But please, spare others.

What good do you think you are doing by placing doubt in their minds? Do you truly believe that you are saving them from something? Are all saved when they hear the Word? No. Read the Parable of the Sower and it will tell you what happens. Are all healed when they hear the Word? No. But some want to make "so-called" scriptural excuses for that. But the reason is the same. Read the Parable of the Sower. There is a song by a rap group, Fort Minor (secular), that is called, "Remember the Name." I am a fan of rap and the first time I heard the song I liked it. But I wished someone would do a Christian Remix because I feed myself music that has Christian lyrics. Lecrae and another gentleman (Sam FranjiONE) have now indeed done separate remixes. Both are good in their own right, and when I hear them, I remember the Name. *"There is no other Name under Heaven given among men whereby we must be saved."* Acts 4:12b.

Now the seventh way that you can be healed, which I will focus on in this chapter, is by the gift of miracles or the gift of healing. These are actually two separate spiritual gifts as listed in 1 Corinthians 12:9-10. It states,

> To another faith by the same Spirit, to another gifts of healing by that one Spirit, to another the working of miracles, to another prophecy, to another distinguishing between spirits, to another speaking

in various tongues, and to still another the interpretation of tongues.

Many Christians are not clear concerning the difference in these two gifts and due to this, they grow weary in well-doing. They lose hope in some cases. The gift of miracles is exactly what it states. A gift given by the Holy Spirit working through a Believer to bring about a miracle. Now all miracles don't have to do with sickness or disease. If you don't believe that, then just ask Moses about the parting of the Red Sea when you get to speak with him in Heaven. But we typically, whether consciously or subconsciously, connect the miraculous to acts of healing. In these cases, someone (Christian or non-Christian) is gravely ill and at death's door. Someone shows up and prays for and speaks God's Word over that person and that person is immediately healed. We have a person in our congregation whom I will not name, but I will briefly share her story. To summarize, she went to the doctor. He pronounced her sick with terminal cancer. Then she had the elders of the church pray over her. When she returned to the doctor, the cancer was completely gone, and she was released. This is an example of the working of the gift of miracles. The healing happened immediately in the face of extreme need (meaning it was terminal).

On the other hand, an example of the gift of healing is when someone is ill and receives prayer and then battles with the disease and against the enemy for a period of time and then is healed. I will use myself for this example. Over four years ago I was diagnosed with stage four metastatic prostate cancer and I was given a few months to live. The technician at

Shands who administered the MRI became overwrought when looking at my results. I could hear him saying, "Oh no, God, please do not let this man go through this." I gave the MRI to my back doctor who very somberly referred me to an oncologist. The oncologist suggested that they perform radiation on the areas in which I had pain and they put me on pills that would reduce my testosterone levels to slow the spread of the cancer. I agreed to take the pills for one year. I did, and at the end of the year the Lord clearly spoke to my spirit and said stop the medication. He did not have to speak very loudly in that one of the side effects of the pills was some serious joint pain. Since then, I have had some localized radiation treatment to address some tissue swelling, etc. But, otherwise, I have had no medication. Now, that is not to say that I oppose taking medication and I'm not saying to do so is anti-faith or wrong. I am just saying that, in this situation, up to this point, this is what God has had me do. I have had to battle with the enemy for four years (anemia, minor pain, and edema). But I still work 40-hour weeks, I still ride my bicycle on rail trails weekly with my wife, and I write what God puts in my heart that He believes may help someone else. As I have previously mentioned herein, the doctor forbade me to ride my bike at first. He believed that my bones would just crumble if I took a serious fall. I have been riding my bike for that entire four plus years and my wife can tell you that I have been thrown on the ground, thrown into trees, and tumbled head over heels down hills, but have not suffered one broken bone. In this, I must give thanks to God, since He does say in Psalm 91:11-12,

For He will command His angels concerning you to guard you in all your ways; they will lift you up in their hands, so that you will not strike your foot against a stone.

And trust me, what it states has been the case. If you would have seen some of the falls, you would understand that the glory is all the Lord's. The angels who He has given me to protect me are very good and diligent at doing their jobs and I thank God for them.

So, that is a summary of both spiritual gifts and examples of each one. Would it be better to have the gift of miracles applied instead of the gift of healing to avoid long-term battle? I would say, "yes." But, know this, that if it had not been for the battle, it is likely that I would not have written this book. My faith would not have been built-up the way that it has been in order that I may pray for healing in the lives of others. *"For to me, to live is Christ and to die is gain."* *Philippians* 1:21.

I truly believe that Paul was forbidden by God from telling of the things that he alludes to seeing in the Third Heaven in 2 Corinthians 12:2-4, because the things he would have shared were so magnificent that there was a legitimate concern that Believers would be unduly influenced by what Paul had seen and they would seek to cross the veil before their allotted time. There could be various issues with this, but the main one is the fact that God is trying to build an army here. He does not need an army in Heaven. He has an army (angels). He needs one here in human flesh but walking in and living by the Holy Spirit to do battle with the enemy on this side of eternity. The temptation in hard times would be to let go and move on, but "to live is Christ." Even Paul himself stated in *Philippians* 1:23. "*I am torn between the two. I desire to depart and be with Christ, which is far better indeed.*" Yet he knew that it was better to continue to "*fight the good fight of faith,*" as stated in 1 Timothy 6:12. That is what we need to do as well. Thank you Lord for that opportunity.

CHAPTER FIVE

—◆—

WHAT CAN AND SHOULD I DO TO GROW IN FAITH?

S mith Wigglesworth had a great healing ministry in England in the early 1900s. He once shared the following statement concerning healing:

> When people are in sickness, you find frequently that they are dense about Scripture. They usually know three scriptures though. They know about Paul's thorn in the flesh, and that Paul told Timothy to take a little wine for his stomach's sake, and that Paul left someone sick somewhere; they forget his name, and don't remember the name of the place, and don't know where the chapter is. Most people think they have a thorn in the flesh. The chief thing

in dealing with a person who is sick is to locate their exact position.

Wigglesworth nailed the problem that most Christians have in trying to obtain their healing. They lack true Bible faith. They have sat in the local church or looked at YouTube, etc. and watched pastors, evangelists, and lay people tell you why, according to the Bible, you can't be healed. They ignore the fact that Jesus healed all who came to Him, the fact that healing is part and parcel of the atonement, *"by His stripes you are healed,"* and the fact that God spent a whole lot of time telling of ways to be healed in the New Testament.

So, you ask, "What are some of the things that I can do or avoid doing to help me grow?"

1. Foremost is to spend time studying healing scriptures in God's Word. This will accomplish two important things. First, it will give you a personal knowledge of what the Bible says about healing. That way you don't have to depend on others to tell you what the Bible says about healing (in their opinion). Second, you will build your faith since faith comes through God's Word.

2. Spend time listening to healing scriptures during some of your down time. I have developed a habit of listening as I go to bed. I listen to *Healing Scriptures* by Pastor John Hagee. Whether awake or asleep the Word is getting into my spirit via the Holy Spirit.

3. Avoid listening to faith killing sermons. There are more than a few pastors who apparently feel that it is their calling from God to create doubt in God's people when it

comes to healing. You don't have to listen to them. Turn them off. As stated in James 1:5-8,

Now if any of you lacks wisdom, he should ask God, who gives generously to all without finding fault, and it will be given to him. But he must ask in faith, without doubting, because he who doubts is like a wave of the sea, blown and tossed by the wind. That man should not expect to receive anything from the Lord. He is a double-minded man, unstable in all his ways.

The words these preachers speak plant seeds of doubt. You find yourself making excuses instead of trusting God and taking Him at His Word.

4. Listen to Christian music. I know that most of us did not grow up listening to Christian music. We sang hymns or praise and worship songs at church and then listened to rock, rap, alternative, or country, etc. the rest of the week. Christian music has evolved and has any type of genre that you can find in secular music. There is one major difference though. The lyrics are Christian and are typically Christ-centric. The words in the songs get into our spirit and our minds, and we meditate on them all day. I know that you, like me, have had a song go over and over in your head and you can't get rid of it. Those words are either God's Words or the words of the world. You are not a worse Christian for listening to secular music. You are just a weaker Christian.

5. Don't hang out with Believers who are consistently dragging you down or speaking words contrary to the Bible. As Proverbs 18:2 states, "A *fool does not delight in understanding, but only in airing his opinions.*" The words that we speak are very important and we need to consistently speak God's Word and listen to God's Word, for as Proverbs 18:21 states, "*Life and death are in the power of the tongue, and those who love it will eat its fruit.*"

6. Keep the Parable of the Prodigal Son in mind. "What has that got to do with healing?" you might ask. What is the central theme to the Prodigal Son to us as Believers? For most times we don't find ourselves in the position of the prodigal, but typically in the position of the eldest son. You know that one who complained to the father that he rarely received anything from him. There is so much meat in this parable, but one of the things that we should remember that is shared relating to not only our divine health but all of God's blessings is in Luke 11:29-31 (see bold),

   But he answered his father, "Look, all these years I have served you and never disobeyed a commandment of yours. Yet you never gave me even a young goat so I could celebrate with my friends. but when this son of yours returns from squandering your wealth with prostitutes, you kill the fattened calf for him!' 'Son, you are always with me," the father said, "and all that is mine is yours."

   The father to the prodigal and our Father in Heaven states to us elder sons and daughters, "*all that is mine is* yours." Someone receives a miraculous healing and you have to battle for yours . . ."all that is mine is yours." Do you truly believe that all God has is yours? If so, then why would we ever doubt His desire to heal us. "*Your will be done on earth as it is in Heaven.*" There is no sickness or disease in Heaven, is there? All that He has is ours. As is stated in Luke 11:11-12,

> What father among you, if his son asks for a fish, will give him a snake instead? Or if he asks for an egg, will give him a scorpion? So if you who are evil know how to give good gifts to your children, how much more will your Father in Heaven give the Holy Spirit to those who ask Him!"

7. Oswald Chambers, in his devotional, <u>Can a Saint Falsely Accuse God?</u> addresses the Parable of the Talents in Matthew. Chambers points out that the gifts which were being referred to in that parable were obviously the gifts of the Spirit and not natural gifts. What Chambers points out is our tendency to blame God if we don't receive something promised to us from His Word. The servant who received the one talent told the Master that he demanded too much from the servant. Chambers points out that the problem here is that the servant was viewing the situation from a fleshly standpoint and not taking a spiritual view. He states that once we have received the Holy Spirit, God expects us to live like we have. Sometimes it is a battle and at other times it seems as if the battle will never cease. But we are told how to war in the Spirit in Ephesians 6:10-20,

Finally, be strong in the Lord and in His mighty power. Put on the full armor of God, so that you can make your stand against the devil's schemes. For our struggle is not against flesh and blood, but against the rulers, against the authorities, against the powers of this world's darkness, and against the spiritual forces of evil in the Heavenly realms. Therefore, take up the full armor of God, so that when the day of evil comes, you will be able to stand your ground, and having done everything, to stand. Stand firm then, with the belt of truth buckled around your waist, with the breastplate of righteousness arrayed, and with your feet fitted with the readiness of the Gospel of peace. In addition to all this, take up the shield of faith, with which you can extinguish all the flaming arrows of the evil one. And take the helmet of salvation and the sword of the Spirit, which is the word of God. Pray in the Spirit at all times, with every kind of prayer and petition. To this end, stay alert with all perseverance in your prayers for all the saints. Pray also for me, that whenever I open my mouth, words may be given me so that I will boldly make known the mystery of the Gospel, for which I am an ambassador in chains. Pray that I may proclaim it fearlessly, as I should.

CHAPTER SIX

TESTIMONIES OF HEALING

A s I have emphasized throughout this book, I truly believe that as Romans 10:17 states, "*Faith comes by hearing and hearing by the word of God.*" Faith does not come through my testimony. The entire New Testament is built upon the Gospel of Jesus Christ and the foundational base of the Gospel of Jesus Christ is the Parable of the Sower. Jesus told the disciples that if they did not understand the Parable of the Sower, they, in turn, would not understand any of the parables. And parables are how Jesus shared the Gospel. What this means is that our faith cannot be constructed on the experiences (testimonies) of others, no matter how wonderful they are. Our experiences should line up with the Word of God, but the Word of God will not necessarily line up with our experiences. We are experiencing a process of growth in God's Kingdom. There is only one person that is Truth – Jesus; only one Way that we can follow – His way; and only one set of instructions that can be trusted explicitly – the Bible, God's Word. You and I can have a lot of good opinions and thoughts that are positive in nature. But none of us can unequivocally state that we are correct and that what we say is the Truth . . . always . . . in all things. That is the basis on which this book is written. If you don't place that kind of trust in God's Word then you will consistently be thwarted in all that you do. Because, as is stated in James 1, you will be a double-minded person, unstable in all that you do.

We should give testimony to the wonderful works which God has performed in our lives for many reasons:

1. He (God) deserves all praise because every blessing comes from Him. The Bible states in James 1:17: "*Every good and perfect gift is from above, coming down from the Father of the Heavenly lights, who does not change like shifting shadows.*"

2. It confirms His Word is still living and active, as stated in Hebrews 4:12. It helps others grasp the fact that God is still saving, delivering, and healing and His Word is still alive.

3. It opens the mind and heart of the unbeliever or the young Believer to the fact that God wants to bless them, as he did the ones who gave their testimony. He will become aware of the fact as stated by Peter in Acts 10:34, "'*I now realize how true it is that God does not show*

favoritism.'" Strictly stated, "God will do for all what He will do for one and vice versa."

BIBLICAL TESTIMONIES

We will look at eight testimonies on healing from scripture and four from individuals of whom I know personally, including myself, dealing with the miraculous, the longer term, and praying for those that were healed. Let's begin with the healings from scripture:

1. Let's begin with the account of the very first healing in scripture. There were no accounts of healing in the scripture until after Noah's Flood. The very first healing technically was where God healed Sarah's womb so that she might conceive Isaac (Genesis 21:1,7). The very first account of healing was to begin the family of the father of faith whose family we have been engrafted into. Without his faith and without this healing there would have been no Jesus, no redemption, and no Christianity. Oh yeah, I suppose you noticed that this was in the Old Testament. How was the healing accomplished? Through the faith of the father of Faith – Abraham. Again, as stated in James 1:17b, *"He never changes or casts a shifting shadow."* And, as stated in Hebrews 13:8, *"Jesus Christ is the same yesterday and today and forever."*

2. The second, also in the Old Testament, that I have chosen is the healing of Naaman of leprosy (2 Kings 5:10-27). I chose this for a number of reasons. One, while Abraham was the father of both the Jewish and Christian faiths, Naaman was a Gentile. He was a Gentile during a day in which there was no reaching out to all men with the Gospel of Jesus Christ. Second, leprosy was considered the worst disease that could be contracted in that day and time. It would have meant complete isolation and ostracization for Naaman, who was an Aramite, or in the present day, a Syrian. The third is the connection between Naaman and the first Gentile healed in the New Testament by Jesus. That would have been the Syrophonecian (Syrian) woman's daughter who was healed from demon possession by Jesus in Mark 7:24-30. She was healed at a time that Jesus' ministry was to the Jews. He was their Messiah and even went as far as calling the woman a "dog." "Dog" was a Jewish phrase used for Gentiles at that time. The woman responded wisely and with great faith and Jesus not only acknowledged her faith, but He healed her daughter. Both situations show that it is not your social setting that determines your access to God's blessings, but rather your faith.

3. Thirdly, let's contrast the healing of two blind men.

Blind man number one was healed in John 9:1-7,

> As he went along, he saw a man blind from birth.
> ²His disciples asked him, "Rabbi, who sinned, this man or his parents, that he was born blind?"

"Neither this man nor his parents sinned," said Jesus, "but this happened so that the works of God might be displayed in him. As long as it is day, we must do the works of him who sent me. Night is coming when no one can work. While I am in the world, I am the light of the world." After saying this, he spit on the ground, made some mud with the saliva, and put it on the man's eyes. [7]"Go," he told him, "wash in the Pool of Siloam." Siloam literally means "sent". So, the man went and washed, and came home seeing.

First, this man was assumed to be sick due to sin (his or someone else's), but Jesus refuted this stating that "neither he nor his parents sinned."

Second, Jesus said that the man was blind so that the works of God might be displayed in him. In other words, he was sick so that Jesus may receive glory and testify to His divinity. Third, the blind man did not, as related, ask for healing. Fourth, Jesus of His own volition made mud with spit and placed it on the man's eyes and then told him to "Go, *wash in the Pool of Siloam.*" The healing was not immediate, and the man would not have been healed if he had refused to go to the Pool of Siloam and wash (see Naaman). Fifth, the man obeyed and came home seeing.

Blind man number two was healed in Luke 18:35-43,

As Jesus approached Jericho, a blind man was sitting by the roadside begging. When he heard the crowd going by, he asked what was happening. They told him, "Jesus of Nazareth is passing by." He called out,

"Jesus, Son of David, have mercy on me!" Those who led the way rebuked him and told him to be quiet, but he shouted all the more, "Son of David, have mercy on me!" Jesus stopped and ordered the man to be brought to him. When he came near, Jesus asked him, "What do you want me to do for you?" "Lord, I want to see," he replied. Jesus said to him, "Receive your sight; your faith has healed you." Immediately he received his sight and followed Jesus, praising God. When all the people saw it, they also praised God.

First, this blind man was viewed as a nuisance by the crowd, but he ignored their opinion and shouted for Jesus to have mercy on him. Second, he not only was tenacious, but also persistent. Third, Jesus took note of his tenacity and persistence and "ordered" that he be brought to Him. Fourth, the man had already shown faith, so all Jesus asked him was what he wanted (which was, of course, to see) and then Jesus simply replied, and the man was "immediately" healed due to his previously displayed faith. Fifth, Jesus received glory and testified to His divinity.

These two separate examples of healing show the following:

   a. Jesus does not always use the same method to heal us or follow the same path to get to a specific destination. The first man did not even request healing. The second did. The first man had to show that he believed. The second man had already shown that he believed. Don't hold God to a certain pattern.

Let God be God. After all, at the end of it all we just desire to be healed.

b. Jesus performed an outward act (preparing and applying the mud) on the first man and then told him what he needed to do to show he believed, but He just replied to the second man's display of faith. Faith can either be an outward declaration or action. What God is looking at is the heart and what comes out of the abundance of the heart. Faith or unbelief.

c. The first man and his family were known, and he appeared to be from a family of questionable character, but the second was unknown and considered inconsequential. It does not matter at what level society sees us nor how they judge us, there is, as stated in Romans 8:1, *"no condemnation in Christ Jesus."*

d. No matter how an act of healing is performed and no matter how long it takes the one who is on the receiving end of that healing, he will glorify God and testify to His divinity.

4. Fourth, let's examine a healing in a most extraordinary circumstance to a most unlikely candidate. As many of you will remember, Jesus was arrested in the Garden of Gethsemane. This account is related in all four Gospels. But the Gospel of John has a twist. In Luke 22:35-37, Jesus intimates that a sword could well be necessary based upon the reaction of the Jewish leaders to Him,

Then Jesus asked them, "When I sent you out without purse or bag or sandals, did you lack anything?" "Nothing," they answered. "Now, however," He told them, "the one with a purse should take it, and likewise a bag; and the one without a sword should sell his cloak and buy one. For I tell you that this Scripture must be fulfilled in Me: 'And He was numbered with the transgressors.' For what is written about Me is reaching its fulfillment."

So, Peter, whom we all know, was not one to be caught short in a fight and made sure that he had a sword with him in the Garden. The account continues in several of the Gospels once Judas and the soldiers and temple officials entered the Garden. As the confrontation escalated, Peter, who was known to be a little hot-headed at times (as some of the rest of us are without the intervention of the Holy Spirit), drew the sword which he had heard Jesus say he should get and proceeded to cut off the high priest servant's ear. The servant was named Malchus.

Jesus could see that the confrontation had the potential to fly out of control at that point and knowing that was not what he was there for, reached out and healed Malchus' ear. In John 18:11, "*Jesus commanded Peter, 'Put your sword away! Shall I not drink the cup the Father has given me?'*" As some have suggested, Jesus did not contradict His own directive to the disciples to obtain a sword, He merely told Peter to put the sword away before the situation got out of hand and turned into what the enemy always desires – chaos. Jesus knew that a man who carried a sword as a deterrent was much like one that carries a gun in our day and age. Whether of good or bad intent, that man was a lot less likely to be attacked. While Jesus foreknew what was going to happen to Him in His trial, punishment, and crucifixion, He still wanted the very best for His disciples. Thus, He told them to make a show of a sword or two to dissuade others from attacking them.

Jesus had healed not only an enemy, but one that He knew represented not only His earthly foes (Pharisees), but also His spiritual foes (Satan, fallen angels, and demons) too. And He did so that He may be able to suffer at their hands and thus accomplish His earthly mission of redeeming mankind. Which He did. Sometimes God does things that may appear to have no reasonable explanation, but in due time, the answer becomes crystal clear, and His wisdom is always far above our wisdom. What would most of us have done in the Garden? Joined in the battle for our Lord and Savior and He would have had to call the angels down to defeat the spiritual enemy, while He handled the physical force. The whole sacrifice of the Lamb of God would have now allowed the enemy (Satan), with all of His chaos, to turn the situation into what the Pharisees and Romans had always desired. They wanted to prove that Jesus and the Disciples were a bunch of insurrectionists, Hell-bent on overthrowing the Pharisees, Chief Priests, and High Council as well as the Roman Government. The Disciples would not have become "Fishers of Men", but rather those "Fished for by Men." At the very least, their testimony would have become secondary. At the worst, they would have been hunted down and killed.

5. Fifth, let's examine what great faith looks like. It may not look exactly like you imagine. There is a story related in both Matthew 8 and Luke 7. It has been said by various theologians that Matthew wrote to the Jews and Luke wrote to the Gentiles (or Greeks). In the accounts of this story in Matthew 8 and Luke 7, there is an apparent discrepancy. These two Gospels are the ones that cover the largest volume of Jesus' life. Matthew has 18,345 words and Luke 19,482 words and Luke's description of this story is a bit longer (223 words) than that of Matthew (199 words).

So, even though Luke was wordier in general it appears that Matthew gave more details in the story of the centurion. Obviously, two witnesses to the same event that give the same details makes what they have recounted sound contrived. This is true in police work, history, and in anything else that has a foundational basis in eyewitness accounts. What one must understand when comparing the two accounts is that one was written by a Jew from a Jewish perspective and one by a Gentile from a Gentile perspective. You might wonder how this makes a difference in the two accounts of this story.

First, remember that from a Jewish perspective to enter a Gentile's house was considered unclean. Thus, there was great focus in Matthew on Jesus not entering the centurion's home. Also, in the Jewish culture if a man of authority sent those that were subject to him to do or say something then they were considered to personally represent him. It was just like he himself had gone. Thus, the reason for the disparity between the two accounts concerning whether or not the centurion himself went to Jesus as Matthew alluded to, but

Luke did not. In Luke's account, it was the Jewish elders and the centurion's friends that came to Jesus. Note that the Jewish elders pleaded with Jesus to come and then escorted Him to the centurion's house. The friends (likely Gentiles) came from the house and by convincing Jesus not to come into the house very diplomatically prevented an incident that would have put Jesus and the elders in violation of Jewish law. But notice that in Matthew's account, since all of these – the Jewish elders and the friends, went to Jesus at the centurion's bequest, it was considered that he himself had gone to Jesus.

It was not just the last statement that the centurion made in Matthew 8:8-9 that revealed the depth of his faith,

> The centurion answered, "Lord, I am not worthy to have You come under my roof. But just say the word, and my servant will be healed. For I myself am a man under authority, with soldiers under me. I tell one to go, and he goes; and another to come, and he comes. I tell my servant to do something, and he does it."

> That was merely the "coup de grace" of the revelation of his faith. The beginning was when it was revealed that he had built the synagogue. This showed that, despite the teachings of Rome, he did not consider Caesar to be a "god" or himself superior to the Jewish people. He actually revered the God of the Jews and was well studied concerning the scripture. Second, was the fact that he knew what a breach of Jewish legal authority Jesus and the other elders entering a Roman centurion's home would be and he honored that by making sure that they did not have to enter even though Jesus was more than

willing to do so. Thirdly, he sent Jewish elders to plead with Jesus, not his Gentile friends. He saved them to send later to make sure that none of the Jews (Jesus nor the elders) entered his home contrary to Jewish law. By this point, Jesus had already been convinced concerning his faith. The centurion had shown that he had a complete grasp on authority and authority is what faith is based on. At that point, the issue of healing had long been settled, but Jesus proclaimed with His words that the servant was healed.

The centurion was not just a man of faith, he was a generous man, a man of humility, and a man of honor. He refused to put others into potentially dangerous situations just to meet his needs. He knew that if Jesus had the authority that he had determined He had, based on the scriptures, there would be no issue concerning healing no matter when or where it took place. That is great faith. Not just strong faith, but great faith.

6. Sixth, we will observe faith under assault by fear. Oftentimes we have heard that faith is the opposite of fear. I have even seen it on t-shirts. Fear is not the opposite of faith. Doubt is. What is the opposite of "to believe" which is another way to say faith? Well of course "to not believe" which is another way to say "doubt" not "fear." I posit that you can be afraid and still operate in great faith and, in fact, the Bible gives great examples of

such. You cannot be in doubt and operate in faith, according to James 1:5-9,

Now if any of you lacks wisdom, he should ask God, who gives generously to all without finding fault, and it will be given to him. But he must ask in faith, without doubting, because he who doubts is like a wave of the sea, blown and tossed by the wind. That man should not expect to receive anything from the Lord. He is a double-minded man, unstable in all his ways. For he states very clearly that we should expect to receive nothing.

On the other hand, the story of Saul (the Apostle Paul) and his bout with blindness and how Ananias was used to heal him as documented in Acts 9 shows how one can be afraid and still act in faith. In the first part of Chapter 9 Saul has an encounter with Jesus who is in the Spirit and is seen by Saul as a very bright light. Saul is not only thrown from the animal that he is riding, but also becomes blind. Jesus in turn identifies Himself to Saul and castigates Saul for persecuting Him (the body of Believers). He then tells Saul to travel into Damascus and that he will tell him what to do once he is there. Saul, now blind, is led by the men with him to Damascus.

Now remember this is the very same Saul who, up until this point, in the Book of Acts has been killing and encouraging the killing of all Believers. I mean, Acts 9:1 speaks of the murderous threats that he has been speaking to the disciples of the Lord. So, this is where we find Ananias enter the picture in Acts 9:10-19,

In Damascus there was a disciple named Ananias. The Lord spoke to him in a vision, "Ananias!" "Here I am, Lord," he answered. "Get up!" the Lord told him. "Go to the house of Judas on Straight Street and ask for a man from Tarsus named Saul, for he is praying. In a vision he has seen a man named Ananias come and place his hands on him to restore his sight." But Ananias answered, "Lord, many people have told me about this man and all the harm he has done to Your saints in Jerusalem. And now he is here with authority from the chief priests to arrest all who call on Your name." "Go!" said the Lord. "This man is My chosen instrument to carry My name before the Gentiles and their kings, and before the people of Israel. I will show him how much he must suffer for My name." So, Ananias went to the house, and when he arrived, he placed his hands on Saul. "Brother Saul," he said, "the Lord Jesus, who appeared to you on the road as you were coming here, has sent me so that you may see again and be filled with the Holy Spirit." At that instant, something like scales fell from Saul's eyes, and his sight was restored. He got up and was baptized, and after taking some food, he regained his strength. And he spent several days with the disciples in Damascus.

As most of us are, Ananias was all fired up to go and minister in obedience to the Lord. Until he was told what was being asked of him. He was being asked to go and pray for the healing of the most notorious murderer of Believers that day.

What Saul was doing would only be eclipsed by what the Roman Emperors would implement, mass murder. Ananias recited his fears to the Lord and then, of course, the Lord let him off the hook, right? No. The Lord just said, "Go!" He gave Ananias a brief explanation and sent him on his way. Now the next thing we see in scripture is Ananias at the house where Saul is staying. But you know the time between his vision of the Lord and his arrival at the house must have been agonizing. For all Ananias knows, he is being sent to his death. The fact that the Lord appeared to him in a vision was fresh, when it first happened, but as time passed you know that Satan assailed him with fear and doubt.

We also know that while Ananias may not have overcome his fear, he overcame his doubt. How do we know that? Because the scripture states that he obeyed and did what the Lord had directed him to do. He went and prayed for Paul, baptized him, and took him to meet with the Lord's disciples in Damascus. He may or may not have been afraid at the time. I assume that as his faith grew and his doubt dissipated the offshoot of doubt, fear dissipated, as well. But he still could have prayed for Paul and Paul be healed of blindness, if he were fearful, but not if he were in doubt that God was able.

There were many other men in the Bible who performed great exploits and acts for the Lord – Moses at the Red Sea, Gideon with the Midianites, David with Goliath, Ananias with Saul, and Jesus at the Cross, just to name a few. Therefore, from the standpoint of healing, it shows that we can, in the face of fear, pray for ourselves or others and still be standing in faith, as long as we don't doubt. *"Faith comes by hearing and hearing by the word of God."*

7. This account of healing, I believe, is one of the most astounding and significant accounts in the Bible. This account happens to be related in the Old Testament and is signified by a full restoration of life and health to a dead man by a dead man. Elisha, whose name in Hebrew means "God is Salvation" was first mentioned in 1 Kings 19 at the point that Elijah, at the direction of the Lord, went to appoint Elisha to take over his ministry of prophecy and instruction with the School of the Prophets.

One can see that Elisha is a well-to-do man as he was plowing with twelve yoke of oxen (24). As you follow the story of Elisha throughout 1 and 2 Kings, it can also be seen that Elisha is a man of tenacity, loyalty, strength (physical and spiritual), and above all, a man of great faith. For in 2 Kings 2, Elisha received a double portion of the spirit of Elijah which was, for all intents and purposes, a double portion of the Spirit of the Lord.

Throughout 2 Kings, Elisha continues to perform many great feats of faith – the multiplication of the widow's oil, raising of the Shunammite woman's son from the dead, the purification of poisonous stew, making an ax head float, feeding 100 men with 20 loaves of bread, the previously reviewed healing of Naaman, and the capturing of the blinded Aramean army and their eventual peaceful release – mighty acts of faith each and every one.

But he saved the best for last. Even after the last, you might say. In 2 Kings 13:14, it states, "When Elisha had fallen sick with the illness from which he would die." After prophesying to King Jehoash and then rebuking him it simply states in 2 Kings 13:20a, "*Elisha died and was buried.*" At this point Elisha had been ministering for about 30 years and was estimated to be in his 50s or 60s. The first issue that comes to mind, at least to my mind, is, "Why didn't his great faith in God raise him up from the sick bed as it had done for others?" I mean, look at all the great deeds and miraculous feats of faith he had performed for others. I believe that the answer can be found in the fourteenth chapter when a band of Moabite raiders threw a dead man into Elisha's tomb and there was still so much power and anointing on Elisha's bones that the man came back to life. If his dead bones could bring a dead man back to life, he certainly could have raised himself up, if he had wanted to. The key is in the statement, "if he had wanted to." As previously stated, we all die. Even the two men that have yet to die (Enoch and Elijah). I believe they will both die while serving as the two witnesses in Revelation 11. Note that one of those men, Elijah, was Elisha's great friend and mentor. A prophet with twice the anointing of Elijah (one who went to Heaven without dying) would most likely have a good grip on what waited for him on the other side of the veil. It appeared that he was tired (he had fallen ill) and had run his race and had chosen to go home. He obviously could have chosen otherwise.

I believe that the very same thing happens and has happened through and to mighty men and women of God throughout the ages. They have had enough faith to continue and to be raised up, but they recognized, as Paul stated in Philippians 1:21, "*To live is Christ, and to die is gain.*" They felt that they had, as the Apostle Paul stated in 2 Timothy 4:7, *"fought the good fight, finished the race, kept the faith."* In other words, they were done and wanted to go home, like Elisha and Paul. I believe, as you grow closer to death your view of the other side becomes clearer. Many great men and women of faith, once they get closer to what is described in scripture as paradise, they choose not to return to the battlefield. That is fine for those that have finished running their race and fighting their fight. But for those of us that are still an active part of God's Army, we need to continue to fight the good fight and stand firm and know, "to Live is Christ." Or, as is so aptly stated in Romans 10:14,

> How, then, can they call on the one they have not believed in? And how can they believe in the one of whom they have not heard? And how can they hear without someone preaching to them?

8. I had intended to finish my accounts of biblical healing with the account of Elisha in the Old Testament. But I felt compelled by the Holy Spirit to include the following account that I touched on previously in Testimony #2. Knowing that the number eight represents New Beginnings makes me feel even more intent on including this story. It is the story of Jesus and the Syrophoenician woman who sought healing for her daughter who was possessed with a demon, as told in Mark 7:24-30,

> Jesus left that place and went to the vicinity of Tyre. He entered a house and did not want anyone to know it; yet He could not keep his presence secret. In fact, as soon as she heard about him, a woman

whose little daughter was possessed by an impure spirit came and fell at his feet. The woman was a Greek, born in Syrian Phoenicia. She begged Jesus to drive the demon out of her daughter. "First let the children eat all they want," He told her, "for it is not right to take the children's bread and toss it to the dogs." "Lord," she replied, "even the dogs under the table eat the children's crumbs." Then He told her, "For such a reply, you may go; the demon has left your daughter." She went home and found her child lying on the bed, and the demon was gone.

While Jesus calls out the Centurion in Matthew 8, as having "great faith," to me, the account of the Syrophoenician woman is one of the most astounding examples of faith in the New Testament. It also was of overt significance in what it signaled. As a Syrophoenician, the woman was essentially a bridge between the Jewish and Gentile peoples. She was from Canaan and of Greek heritage. Canaan, the land of giants and ungodly residents that God cast out so that the Israelites could occupy the Promised Land. She was not only not accepted (see Samaritans/Gentiles). She was hated (see Canaanites). She was part of the primary peoples that were enemies of the Most High. She lived in Tyre. If you will reference Ezekiel 28, you will see it is the King of Tyre to which Satan was compared and it is there in Ezekiel 28 that the end of Helel, the archangel, was unfolded. From that point on he was Satan, the Adversary, the Dark Lord. He essentially was the spiritual King of Tyre. So, this gives a little background into what this woman faced. To call it an uphill climb is a vast understatement. For Jesus to heal this woman, given her heritage and ethnicity, was totally contrary to Jewish belief and culture. This account, along with the account of the healing of the Centurion, showed the beginnings of the shift of the Kingdom of God, not only toward the Gentiles, but the actual shift away from the Age of Israel to the Church Age.

To begin with, Jesus did not want anyone to know that He was present in the area. He had obviously gone there for a specific reason. I believe that reason was to encounter this woman and to do battle with the demons in what had once been Satan's headquarters. Much the same, as He eventually takes the disciples to Caesarea Philippi to proclaim full war on the Dark Kingdom. The encounter did not begin well for the woman. She fell at his feet and begged for healing for her daughter. Note the differences between her and the Centurion. The Centurion had a group of advocates from the Jewish synagogue. Not only did she lack an advocate, but she was also of a hated race, was a woman, and was disturbing Jesus when He had ordered to be left alone. If Las Vegas were setting odds on her daughter being healed by Jesus, she would have been the longest of long shots. Jesus then proceeded to refer to her as a "dog," thus revealing what the Jews thought of not just Gentiles, but Canaanites, the enemies of the Most High. Remember who Jesus was and is. Yes, the Most High Himself. I mean, the Samaritans were hated. But how did Jesus treat the woman at the well during another intentional meeting? With kindness – even in her sin. This woman was called a "dog" and was told that He would not heal her daughter.

It was then that the woman showed an almost unfathomable resilience. Most of us, by that time, would have walked away angry and defeated. But this woman persevered by telling Jesus that while she may yet be considered by Him and His disciples as a "dog," that even literal dogs eat the crumbs that fall from the tables of their Masters. She not only did not shy away from being called a "dog," but she continued by calling Jesus her Master. This was the faith that Jesus needed to see and hear in order for her daughter to be healed. His power was present. It always was and is. It was the connection of faith that needed to be ensured. Based upon the history of all the peoples involved, Jesus had to have her show a strong faith connection. The Centurion had already done so before his encounter with Christ by his actions toward the Jewish people. He showed that he understood that they were God's people and that Jesus had come to minister to them. His faith combined with his humility had already been displayed. The woman had shown nothing but a desire to have her daughter healed. Desire is not a replacement for faith. Sometimes we mistake desire for faith. But they are not the same. The connection between our need and His power must be through faith not desire or anything else. Jesus, by His comments, was not trying to be mean or cruel as some have interpreted. No. He was pressuring her to determine if she indeed had what the Centurion had – both faith and humility. She had both and showed Him that she did. Sometimes we misinterpret God's actions as unkind or even mean. For example, in questions like, "Why do I have this or that disease or problem and that person never has any issues?" First off, we never know what others may be or have been dealing with. But finally, there are times that God must push us – like a Master Sergeant does his troops in training. Are his actions kind or mean? At first flush, one might reply that they are mean. But when the battle begins and the difficult training experiences work to save the soldier's life, the answer becomes clear. The actions of the Sergeant were indeed kind and loving to the point that they worked to save the life of that soldier. We too, are in a war, and at times God's methods and timing may seem unkind or, yes, seem even mean to us. But when the enemy strikes we must fight for our very lives or the lives of our loved ones, like the Syrophoenician woman. It is then, and only then, that we see the truth and understand.

I have covered various aspects of being healed through the biblical examples. Each example shows at least one, if not several, potential stumbling blocks, and one, if not several, potential pathways to obtain our healing based upon the stories of those who experienced healing in the scriptures. We will now look at personal healing accounts and see what parallels there are with those that we reviewed from scripture.

PERSONAL TESTIMONIES

These accounts of healing have been shared with me for placement in this book by the following individuals: Me, Pastor Seth Shaw, Pastor Wayne Godsmark, Lisa Thornton, and Amanda Hunt. I want to thank them for their selflessness in allowing me to share their experiences. I have not dictated any aspect of the accounts other than persuading the individuals to simply allow the Holy Spirit to guide and direct them in what they share. Some of the accounts focus solely on the miraculous, while some include the part that modern medicine played in the healing. Some of the accounts are from the view of the healed and some are from the view of those whom God used to heal.

All accounts glorify God and promote the fact that God wants us well. We all may get there in different ways. But the finality of what God wants us to focus on is the same as that first personal encounter in Matthew 8 when the leper said to Jesus, "Lord if you are willing you can make me clean," and Jesus responded to the leper by reaching out and touching him while stating, "I am willing." I am willing enough to reach out to you and touch you, a leper, who not only is unclean, but who carries a highly contagious, unhealable (by human standards in that day) skin disease. These accounts, as desired, are focused on one thing. By whatever means necessary, "I am still willing."

My Testimony

I am going to share a major healing experience that I have experienced. I was the type of guy who did not go to the doctor much and the last time that I had spent a night in the hospital before being diagnosed with cancer was when I was in my senior year of high school. I had food poisoning right before my final high school football game. We had a very good team (we finished ranked 3rd in the State in our classification) and I proposed in my heart to play the game. I did and I played both offensive guard and middle linebacker as I had all year. That was in 1969. Up until I began to deal with some of the side issues associated with the cancer diagnosis that I received in May of 2018, that was the last time I was in the hospital, other than just a visit or two to the emergency room and one outpatient surgery for an inguinal hernia.

In May of 2018, I had a right hip replacement surgery. After the surgery, while going through rehabilitation, I began to experience sciatic nerve pain in my left leg which was seriously impacting my ability to stand or walk except for a very minimal length of time. I was referred by my hip doctor to a back doctor in the same facility. The back doctor sent me in for MRIs and CAT scans. The first indication that there was a problem was when I heard the technician, who was studying my MRI results, begin to almost weep while reviewing the scans. He, of course, said that I would have to see my doctor for the analysis. When I returned to see my back doctor he was very somber and told me that what he had to tell me would be life altering and that he wanted to refer me to an oncologist immediately. After heading south toward Gainesville, because the oncologist in Lake City was booked, I was called and told to turn around and come back to Lake City and they would see me immediately.

I arrived at the oncologist's office and he saw me right away. The doctor said that the diagnosis was prostate cancer and it had metastasized throughout my body. He stated that they were going to treat me but he gave me about a month to live. God gave me great peace. Throughout my Christian walk I had believed that God heals, and I had studied healing and confessed that "by Jesus' stripes, I am healed," for many years. But now the rubber was meeting the road. A day or so later Jodée, my wife, was diagnosed with skin cancer. We were under attack. By God's grace, the type of cancer Jodée was diagnosed with was easily removed and she has had no further issues. I was placed on medications that were basically meant to chemically reduce my testosterone levels to the level of castration. I had prayed about it and told the doctor that I would take the medication for one year and then I would personally reassess the situation. Of course, they were not convinced that I would be alive in a few months, much less a year. But off we went on this new journey.

The Holy Spirit rose up within me and my confession with regards to my healing in Christ got to the point that it was aggravating to some. But I can attest to the fact that a person fighting for his own life doesn't care how others respond or think. I didn't care. I refused to call it "my cancer." I would state that I had been diagnosed with cancer not that I had it. When people would ask how I was, I would respond to them that I was healed by Jesus' stripes and that, based on the fact that the Holy Spirit which indwelled me was the same Spirit that raised Christ from the dead, He was quickening (giving life to) my mortal body (1 Peter 2:24 and Romans 8:11). I followed what the scripture said. I had the elders pray for me. I had groups of prayer warriors pray for and with me. When I was afraid, I told my wife and she prayed for me. I never hid fear. I had learned many years ago that fear and sin grow in darkness but fade in the light.

This was not a miraculous healing. This healing was and is a war. After a year, I felt that God told me to stop taking the medication. Jodée had audibly heard God say in her ear that this was not a death sentence for me. This had been confirmed by three separate individuals. The enemy would not kill me by way of this diagnosis of cancer. God would be glorified. The oncologist was not happy when I told him I would not continue taking the medication. He meant well, but we argued with me telling him that I was trusting Christ Jesus. He could not fathom what I was doing. My radiation oncologist, on the other hand, understood, as he is a Believer. I have had radiation treatments five to six times on various areas of soft tissue in my body. Due to prayer (thanks so much to all the prayer warriors), I have had absolutely no side effects from the radiation. I have worked four 10-hour days per week from the day I was diagnosed and continue working the same hours today. This was true from the beginning through all my radiation treatments other than the few times that I was in the hospital.

I have had bouts of iron deficiency anemia and double bacterial pneumonia which have landed me in the hospital and put me on what I felt was death's door a couple of times. But God redeemed me, brought me out of the hospital, and continued healing me. I have had my left hip replaced. I was told by my hip doctor that he saw a spot while doing surgery which he believed was cancerous and that I needed to have the bone treated with radiation after I got out of the hospital. I went to my radiation oncologist to set this up. He had reviewed the results of the tests and asked me what I was there for. He stated that he reviewed the scans and that there was no cancer in the bone. It was clean. The hip doctor who has been in practice for over 40 years was incredulous. He said that it had to be cancerous. It wasn't. God is faithful.

It has been around four and a half years now and I am getting better every day. I still work four 10-hour work weeks; we bicycle around 20 miles every weekend; and God and I don't have nearly as many arguments about how nice a miraculous healing would be. He and I are great friends. I don't have to be religious. I have yelled, cried, fought demons and fallen angels and fear, and did it all in the name of Jesus and to His glory. It is nice to have a miracle to share and for everything to be gone immediately. But there are miracles and there is healing. I have done all that I know to do and then, I have continued to stand. I am still standing. Because He is still God. God has been faithful and by Jesus' stripes I am healed.

Pastor Seth Shaw's Testimony

It was October 3, 2012; we were on our second day of a conference at church. As our guest speaker was sharing, I was captivated by his testimony. He was sharing that God is still moving in powerful ways by His healing power. The healing power of God had been something I had been interested in for quite some time. For nearly two years, God had been revealing scripture to me that dealt in the area of healing. However, at the same time, I was frustrated as I had prayed for many people but saw nothing happen.

This night something happened; though I cannot fully explain why it was different, it built a faith in me that God would soon use. The next day, while at work (I was a phone/internet guy at the time), I was at a customer's house. The man had just gotten in a motorcycle wreck and had broken ribs and a broken shoulder. He was laid up in bed and apologized as his mobility was limited. While he could stand up, the broken ribs made it very slow. However, he could not move his shoulder and was set to get surgery on it.

As I am hooking up his internet, I feel/hear the Holy Spirit speak to me, "Pray for him." Naturally, doubt began to form, and I responded, "God, he was in a motorcycle wreck; he is supposed to hurt." God then replies, "What does that matter to me? Pray for him." After a back-and-forth argument with God, I finally submitted as God said, "What do you have to lose?"

I asked the guy if I could pray for him and lay hands on him, and he agreed, but what would happen next caught us both by surprise. I have no power, but I believe the Word of God is full of power. I then began to speak the Word of God and, in obedience to His Word, said, "In the name of Jesus, broken ribs, I command you to be healed."

As I prayed, it felt like low-voltage electricity flowed through my fingertips. I then asked how he felt. His response was, "it felt as if a breath of fresh air entered my lungs," and then, with ease, he sat up.

He sat with his arm held tight to his side, and I asked him about his shoulder. As he tried to move it, I watched pain grip his face. I then asked if I could lay hands on his shoulder and pray. I continued praying scripture over him and speaking the same general words, "Broken shoulder, in the name of Jesus, I command you to be healed."

As I said this prayer, I felt something move like his bones in the palm of my hand. I then asked him how he felt. With zero pain, he moved his shoulder in full motion and canceled his shoulder surgery.

I wish I understood all there was to understand about healing. Why are some prayers answered just as you pray and others differently? However, I will not allow my lack of understanding to keep His Word from moving. Since that day, I have seen hundreds of healings and miracles—more than I can count. Never stop declaring the truth because God's grace is more than enough!

That day I learned fear would hold you back, but faith will lead to the impossible.

Pastor Wayne Godsmark's Testimony

The author, my friend, Bob White, asked me to write out a testimony about God's healing power. Wow, where do I start?

Starting in 1998 (when I turned forty), my body seemed to start falling apart. I had developed pancreatitis and spent a total of approximately ninety days in three different hospitals.

The first night at the emergency room, we kept waiting for answers. However, it wasn't until the next day that the doctor explained that I had pancreatitis and my blood was so thick that they were shocked that it continued to flow through my veins. During my stay in hospital #1, I developed blood clots which broke loose and traveled to my lungs. Little did I know, this was only the beginning of a very long illness. When the doctors at hospital #1 ran out of options, they sent me to hospital #2. It was here that I became septic and was told it could be lethal if I didn't respond to treatment. However, once again, God brought me through this set back as well. Finally, after much advice from all the medical teams I had been assigned to so far, I was sent to hospital #3. It wasn't until my third hospital visit that I learned of the extensive damage that had occurred by all the gastric juices released from my explosive pancreas. The doctor explained that it was like a chemical burn on the inside of my abdominal cavity. My sugar, triglycerides, cholesterol and just about everything else they could measure was off the charts. For example, my triglycerides were the highest recorded at the hospital of 9,000 PLUS.

Well, miracles still happen. As a minister, I had a whole lot of praying friends. Word spread quickly! They prayed remotely and many came to lay hands on me, anoint me with oil, and pray the prayer of faith over me. The doctors were at a loss which is the reason I ended up in three hospitals. The first two teams of doctors told us that surgery was not an option but the third announced to us that it would be the only thing that would save my life. My wife expressed her concern because the two other hospitals had said that surgery would kill me. This doctor calmly looked at my wife and said, "Ma'am, you know the medical books that those doctors read from? Well, I wrote them." He was a world renown expert on the pancreas. He explained that surgery wasn't optional but there would be a window of time that he would need to wait for. We waited for one week, still wondering . . . when? Finally, he announced it was time! After the surgery I was left with six drains installed in my abdomen. I don't remember just how long they were left in, but I do remember when they were removed...the pain was tremendous!! There was no anesthesia given, just the strong jerks of a few determined nurses. Nevertheless, God continued to lead me out of this very dark valley. Upon leaving the third hospital, I had lost 100 pounds! I looked like a dead man walking. It was only through the grace of God that I was given life again!

Twenty-four years later I am still testifying of God's healing power. Yes, God uses science, medicine, and doctors, or whatever tools he chooses. But beyond it all, it is by his supernatural power that healing is provided to the sick. In addition, we learn that his amazing grace is more than sufficient to get us through any and everything life throws our way.

I also want to testify of the healings God has provided for many in our church in Live Oak. We have laid hands on many people throughout our eighteen years of ministry there, and we have seen God do amazing things: cancers, medical conditions, physical pain, ... disappearing out of people's bodies! Some instantly, some progressively, but all miraculously! Yes, my friend, Jesus Christ, the same yesterday, today and forever more.

I encourage you to study the promises of healing found in God's Word. Find them, quote them, and stand upon them. Have faith and believe those promises are for you.

Wayne has also authored "He, Not It! Which is about the Holy Spirit and how He works for, in, and through us on a daily basis.

Pastor Wayne Godsmark, Christ Central ,
wayne@christcentral.org

Isaiah 53:5; Matthew 8:17; Matthew 10:8; James 5:13-15; 1 Peter 2:24; 1 Corinthians 12:7-9

Lisa Thornton's Testimony

In December 2010, I was told to get my first mammogram because I was 40 years old.

I went for the first mammogram the same month, same year. My results came back suspicious, and I was told I needed a biopsy. This being my first time for a mammogram, I have to be honest and say, "Yes, I was very nervous." God was with me!

Having a suspicious result, I was told I would have to have a mammogram every six months for two years. In June 2011, I went for my second mammogram, and all was good.

On December 8, 2011, I went for my third mammogram, I was told everything was good – no change.

On March 4, 2012 (it was a Sunday evening). I was bathing. Out of the blue, I looked down and saw a lump on my left breast. Surprisingly, I was very calm. My only thought was, "Well, that's weird!" God was with me!

I called my doctor's office the next day and we got the process started on other tests, a mammogram, and an ultrasound.

I was told I would need another biopsy on March 19, 2012. I had my first visit with a surgeon on March 22, 2012. I had my biopsy done. The lump was removed.

On March 28, 2012, I went for my follow-up visit with my surgeon and waited nervously with my husband for the surgeon to come into the room. I was on the table and my husband was sitting in the chair. The surgeon came into the room and said, "Good morning" to us both, shook my husband's hand, and then the surgeon rubbed my arm. After a few minutes he said it was breast cancer. My husband was in tears. I just laid back on the table and covered my eyes with both hands. I don't remember if any words were said. After a minute or two, I sat up and my ONLY concern was, "How will this affect my daughters and my granddaughter." That was the very first question that came out of my mouth. I was told I would need 33 treatments of radiation and hormone medication for five years and mammograms every six months.

On April 12, 2012, I had surgery to remove some lymph nodes from around my left armpit to be tested. The results were negative. God was with me!

I began making phone calls to my female family members to see if any of them on either side had ever had breast cancer. I was told "No!" on both sides. I was the first in my family. God was with me!

After having more tests done, I began my first radiation treatment on May 30, 2012. I completed my treatments and began my first hormone medication two weeks later, on July 26, 2012. I was having very bad side effects and I told my oncologist I would never take another medication. Well, in October of 2012, I began a new medication that worked very well for me. About five and one-half years later, I was told I could stop the medicine. Roughly two years ago I was told I could begin having mammograms once every year instead of every six months (there were a few bumps in the road with mammograms over the years). God was with me!

After hearing the words, "breast cancer," never, even until this day, did I ever ask why. I knew that God had allowed me to see the lump and revealed it to me, not to hurt me, but for the purpose of allowing me to share my faith in Him and to experience His healing through doctors, science, and medication. When I started telling family, friends, and ladies in support groups my story, I always gave God all the glory. All my faith was, is, and will always be in my Heavenly Father.

I have now been free from cancer for over 10 years. God was with me! God is with me! God will always be with me!

Amanda Hunt's Testimony

(as shared in her book Walking in the Miraculous)

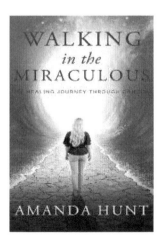

Do You Believe in Miracles?

"*You have cancer.*" Before Amanda Hunt's mind could even process what the doctor said, her body reacted. She nearly dropped the phone, trembling in fear, as tears flooded her hazel eyes. She could hear his words but barely comprehend them. She felt a heaviness, almost a sense of being suffocated. She could hardly breathe, much less speak. Amanda just fell into her husband's arms. He pulled her close but Jonathan didn't say a word. His embrace brought her a sense of comfort, but she could feel the uncertainty he battled as well.

The week prior, Amanda celebrated her 38th birthday. Being two years shy of 40 felt old to her at the time, but after hearing those three dreaded words, suddenly 38 felt incredibly young.

As a mother of five school-aged children, including triplet pre-teen daughters, Amanda ran a busy household. She and Jonathan volunteered on the music team at their church and enjoyed their full life. She didn't want to die, but she also didn't want the radical surgery she was told she needed—as a first step. Jonathan and Amanda had only been married three years and looked forward to a long future together.

Amanda didn't know what to do, but there was one person she knew of who was unexplainably healed of a similar, incurable diagnosis. She reached out to him at church to learn about his story. *If Mr. Lee was miraculously healed, maybe I could be too*, she thought.

After their brief meeting, Amanda took every word Mr. Lee said to heart. His faith was like none she'd encountered. She wanted to be like that. She wanted her life to be a miraculous testimony. But the next few months proved to be the most difficult of her life as she fought the roller coaster of emotion that ensued. It seemed that as her faith rose to a new level, the darkness and fear did too. In the midst of her struggle, several divine appointments came along her path who encouraged her and taught her what she needed to make it through. What happened as a result was nothing short of a miracle. Even the doctors could not believe their own eyes!

Now, a year later, Amanda is completely healed and whole. At her one-year checkup the doctor told her, "I don't even see a scar. If I didn't know your history, I would not think you even had a biopsy." Not only is the cancer completely gone with no medical intervention, but there isn't even a single scar from her many biopsies. Amanda went from a place of complete overwhelm to Walking in the Miraculous.

CHAPTER SEVEN

———◆———

THOUGHTS ABOUT OUR ULTIMATE HEALING BY JODÉE WHITE

I noticed one thing my husband failed to mention in this book. There is yet another aspect of healing which needs to be addressed. Our ultimate healing!

Scripture states in Hebrews 9:27,

> And as it is appointed unto men once to die, but after this the judgment:

Hebrews Chapter 9 speaks of the blood of Jesus. It speaks of the difference between the blood of goats and calves which were shed to cleanse the sins of the people before Jesus was crucified. But scripture states in this chapter that Jesus entered the Most Holy Place once for all by his own blood, thus obtaining eternal redemption for us all. The blood of the animals that were killed prior to Jesus' crucifixion was sprinkled on those who were ceremonially unclean and sanctified them so that they were outwardly clean. How much more, then, will the blood of Christ, who through the eternal Spirit offered himself unblemished to God, cleanse our consciences from acts that lead to death, so that we may serve the living God.

It is our acceptance of Jesus and what he did which appropriated our sins being wiped away by His blood. You see, Jesus put away sin by his own sacrifice. Jesus took all the sins of the world upon Himself all at one time and that all (His Children) who wait and watch for His return, to them (again, this speaks of His Children), He will appear the second time without sin unto salvation.

Wow! This says a lot. It says much more within the chapter than what I just put in writing. You ought to read it all. It really clarifies a lot to the sinner about Jesus' saving grace.

So it is of utmost importance to understand, that at that moment when we are appointed to die, we, the Believer (those who are saved by grace and whose sins are covered by His blood) will cross over to eternity with Jesus and at that moment we will each receive our "ultimate healing."

Again, we will all die at some point. Even the two mentioned in the Bible, Enoch and Elijah, which were taken up to Heaven, they must die as well. I believe they are the two witnesses mentioned in Revelation 11:8-13.

In Heaven there is no sickness and no death (Revelation 21:4)... only life everlasting with our Creator and Heavenly Father and with our Lord and Savior, Jesus the Anointed One.

My husband, Bob White, fought the good fight to the end. I believe, because of and through the prayers of many (our friends, family members, and others of whom we did not know) and because of our full faith and trust in God that God extended Bob's life beyond the doctors' imaginations. Bob should have, according to the doctors, died nearly five years ago when he was diagnosed with stage 4 metastatic prostate cancer.

Bob has received his ultimate healing.

HE IS HEALED AND WITH JESUS TODAY!!

EPILOGUE

Herein I have shared what God's Word has to say about healing. I have shared the various aspects including why we get sick, why we don't get healed, how to receive healing, and how to grow in your faith to receive healing. I have also shared some biblical accounts of healing and some personal testimonies. This is far from an exhaustive theological treatise on healing, but I have not written this to cover every point in scripture or even every major point in scripture with regards to healing. I have written this book to share a basic knowledge of biblical healing, so that people can grasp enough of God's Word relative to healing to understand that God not only can heal us, but rather that He wants to heal us. It is His divine will for us to be healed.

Understand that God does not see things the way you and I see them. Unless, of course, we are moving in the Holy Spirit. As we all should understand, while sins are of different proportions to us, i.e., murder compared to telling a lie or stealing compared to gossiping, this is not true of the sin when it encounters God's grace and is covered by His blood. All sin is the same. It does not take more of Jesus' blood to cover the sin of murder than to cover the sin of lying. This is true of all sin. God sees sin as sin as sin, whereas we see different tiers of sin. The same can be related to healing. By now, my hope is that you understand that healing is part and parcel of your redemption and your salvation (to be made whole). So, just as we see some sins as more serious and severe than we do other sins, we see disease and sickness the same way. For instance, no one views a cold the same as they do cancer or a headache the same as diabetes, but God does. To Him, there is no difference. They are all sicknesses and diseases which emanate from the depths of Hell. The stripes that Jesus took on His back for your healing are no different for a cold than they are for cancer. The difference is in our eyes and is related to what we perceive as the end result. A battle with a cold is not likely to kill you. But there are a lot of people that cancer has taken out. That is where the rubber meets the road for us. Just as you can trust that Jesus' blood will cover the most heinous of sins, His stripes will cover the most severe disease or sickness, as easily as they will a headache. Only believe.

"Let His will be done on earth as it is in heaven," we pray. Are there any sick, diseased, infirmed, demon harassed or possessed in Heaven? Emphatically, the answer is, "no." Will there be people dying in New Jerusalem? Well, of course not. Revelation 21:4 states, "He will wipe every tear from their eyes. There will be no more death or mourning or crying or pain, for *the old order of things has passed away.*" Then why do we, as the Body of Christ, continually wrestle with what His will is with regards to healing. You can keep on saying, "well everyone is not healed" from now until Jesus returns and all you will do is crush your own faith and the faith of others. Is everyone saved? No. Does God want everyone saved? Yes. You know He does. Is healing an aspect of our salvation? Yes. Then why do those in the Body of Christ twist God's will, desire, and Word when everyone is not healed, to explain it away. But they don't make the same effort when everyone is not born again?

Many will say, "People still die." I agree with the obvious. And deteriorating health is involved with death in many, if not most, of those cases of death. This includes Believers as well as non-believers. Is this God's best for us? No. But we live in a world that has not yet been completely redeemed physically. We have been redeemed spiritually. This aspect of our redemption culminated at the cross and then the first step of our physical healing began with the resurrection. But we will not experience the final redemption of our physical bodies until the rapture or the "catching away." Many people are not good stewards of their bodies and then they act surprised when ill health plagues them in their older years. This is not meant to be a condemnation of any of us. I, myself, am older and I have had my share of health issues. But I still believe that God will restore what the "cankerworm and locusts have eaten." What Satan has stolen from me, I demand back in Jesus' Name, which includes any aspect of my health that I may struggle with. In order to be an overcomer or more than a conqueror there has to be something to overcome or conquer. Caleb, when he was 85 years old, stated in Numbers 14:10-11,

> Now behold, as the LORD promised, He has kept me alive these forty-five years since He spoke this word to Moses, while Israel wandered in the wilderness. So here I am today, eighty-five years old, still as strong today as I was the day Moses sent me out. As my strength was then, so it is now for war, for going out, and for coming in.

As I stated, Caleb was 85 years old. He had been in the wilderness for 45 years and was, as he stated, just as strong as the day he went out. God's best for us is that when our time on this Earth is up, that as he did with Moses, Elisha, and many others – He will just call us home. Keep in mind there is no need to fear death for death has been stripped of all its power. As Paul stated in 1 Corinthians 15:55, "*Where, O death, is your victory? Where, O death, is your sting?*"

That being said, I have been healthy, and I have been unhealthy, and I prefer being healthy. I have been well, and I have been sick, and I prefer to be well. Finally, I have been in severe pain, and I have been pain-free, and I much prefer to be pain-free. I am sure this is the stance that most everyone would take. The healthy, well, and pain-free option is what God offers. "Oh, yeah," some will say, "Where does God say that?" As is stated in Romans 8:11, "*And if the Spirit of Him who raised Jesus from the dead is living in you, He who raised Christ from the dead will also give life to your mortal bodies because of His Spirit who lives in you.*" Does the Holy Spirit live in you?

Yes, if you are a Believer. Then this verse clearly states that the Holy Spirit will give life to your mortal body. Then those who mock, and scoff will say, "Well, of course He keeps us alive. But that doesn't say anything about healing." If they would examine the scriptures past their biases, they would find out that the Greek word for "life" used here is zóopoieó, which literally translated means, "to give life to, to make alive, to quicken." This does not allude to power to keep you alive. This alludes to the same power that raised Christ from the dead that lives in you. It quickens or restores life too. What happens to a sick part of your body that is healed? It has "life" restored to it.

It is obvious naturally as well as spiritually. The second that you begin to be unhealthy, sick, or in pain, your body immediately begins to fight against what is causing the problem. The Word of God gives you the weapons to fight in the spirit-realm. As stated in Ephesians 6:12, "*We war not against flesh and blood, but against principalities, powers, darkness, and spiritual evil in the heavenly realm.*" Those weapons include faith, the name of Jesus, the blood of Jesus, God's Word, and praying in the Spirit. These are the weapons that you may choose to use, if you have knowledge, understanding, and wisdom that comes only from God. But as stated in Hosea 4:6a, "*My people are destroyed for a lack of knowledge, because you have rejected knowledge, I will also reject you.*" In so many words, since you did not take time to study God's Word and learn His concepts of knowledge, God says that when you come calling out to Him, there is no foundation for you to stand on to fight or no premise for Him to fight for you. We can't ignore the instructions that God has so graciously passed down for us to use as guidance and wisdom in our lives and then expect to deal with spiritual issues successfully. If a person is a spiritual baby, God will take care of that person using some other individual who has knowledge. But if you are one that has rejected God's knowledge, by ignoring it or worse, mocking or scoffing at it, then you are on your own. Sickness is based in the spirit-realm. It has been concocted by demons and fallen angels in the darkness and is from the pit of Hell. Read Psalm 91. You will not only get a running list of destructive diseases, but you will see how ultimate protection is from the Most High. God does not start to redeem you when you go to Heaven. You were completely redeemed when you accepted Jesus as your Savior and made Him Lord of your life.

No doubt we have an enemy that wants to destroy us as stated in John 10:10 by Jesus,

> The thief does not come except to steal, and to kill, and to destroy. I have come that they may have life, and that they may have it more abundantly.

This is a war. We are under attack. Physically, mentally, emotionally, spiritually and in any other way that the enemy can attack us, he will. God has given us mighty weapons of warfare. We are seen by those who fight us as the Children of God, as mighty warriors. They try to make us see ourselves as weak, feeble, inadequate, flawed, spineless worms. Why? Because a worm does not give much of a fight, but a warrior does. So, they whisper lying deceptions into your ear or in the ear of someone who will share it with you or preach it to you.

That way faith will not arise. Double mindedness always destroys faith (see James 1). If you run a race or fight a fight, just because you fall or are knocked down would you say, "Well this just must be God's will and so I will stay here." No! You get up and continue to run the race or fight the fight.

As I shared with one of my four daughters, when I was fighting and losing a long battle with an addiction/disease. I asked her, "Let's say that you and I run to Jacksonville (represents healing/deliverance) from another town, but the terrain is very, very, very rough. What if you get to Jacksonville and you have fallen twice and I get to Jacksonville and I, on the way, fell 1,000 times, but I get up every time and keep running. When I get to Jacksonville, which one of us is in Jacksonville more? "Neither!" she replied. "We both are in Jacksonville." "What would have kept me from getting to Jacksonville?" I asked. "What are you getting at?" she asked. If I had not gotten up and continued to run every time I fell, I would never have gotten there. But since I got up every time I fell, I eventually arrived there too and was there just as much as you were. I later, after a long hard fight, was completely and immediately set free from this addiction/disease. The battle was long. The fight was hard. But the victory in this battle was instantaneous and conclusive. And all the glory is given to God because I wouldn't have won without Him. Because He heals . . . All Who Came to Him.

About The Author

THIS IS BOB WHITE'S SECOND book. His first published work is *Unseen War* which is the first of a trilogy of the *Unseen Series*. His wife, Jodée White is currently completing the series – the second book of the series being *Unseen Soldiers* (of which Bob began writing), and the third book being *Unseen Church*. Bob recently went to his home in Heaven to be with his Lord and Savior Jesus on January 16, 2023.

Bob was born in Fort Myers, Florida, was raised on a north Florida farm in White Springs, Florida, and he last resided in Lake City, Florida with his wife of nearly 17 years.

Bob was married to Jodée White in 2006. Together they have five children – Bob has four daughters – Heather, Hilary, Haley, and Hunter, and Jodée has one son – Zachary..

He was by profession a civil engineer. He worked in the field of water resources at an engineering firm in Lake City, Florida.

Many years ago, Bob was licensed to preach by the Southern Baptist Church, had served on the mission field in Mexico and Guatemala, and had served as a leader for the section of Youth for Christ in the local high schools in Brownsville, Texas. Bob was an active member of his church serving in whatever capacity he could.

Bob felt compelled to write *All Who Came to* Him by the inspiration of the Holy Spirit. His desire and purpose in writing this book was to help others to understand the biblical principles from the written Word of God in order that they may receive their divine healing. Bob's desire was also to teach others that it is God's desire and will to heal all who come to Him. That by hearing the Word of God they may know God's will for their lives by the move of the Holy Spirit – that, by Jesus' stripes they are healed – whether it be physical, spiritual, or any other type of healing.

Website: **GENC1V3.com**

Made in the USA
Columbia, SC
06 October 2023